HISTORY IN DEPTH

THE AMERICAN WEST

Derek Wise

Head of Liberal Studies, Edlington Comprehensive School

Nelson

Thomas Nelson and Sons Ltd
Nelson House   Mayfield Road
Walton-on-Thames   Surrey
KT12 5PL   UK

51 York Place
Edinburgh
EH1 3JD   UK

Thomas Nelson (Hong Kong) Ltd
Toppan Building 10/F
22A Westlands Road
Quarry Bay   Hong Kong

Thomas Nelson Australia
102 Dodds Street
South Melbourne
Victoria 3205   Australia

Nelson Canada
1120 Birchmount Road
Scarborough Ontario
M1K 5G4   Canada

© Derek Wise 1984

First published by Macmillan Education Ltd 1984
(under ISBN 0-333-35098-7)

This edition published by Thomas Nelson and Sons Ltd 1992

ISBN 0-17-435078-3
NPN 9 8 7 6 5 4 3

All rights reserved. No paragraph of this publication may be
reproduced, copied or transmitted save with written permission or
in accordance with the provisions of the Copyright, Design and
Patents Act 1988, or under the terms of any licence permitting
limited copying issued by the Copyright Licensing Agency,
90 Tottenham Court Road, London W1P 9HE.

Any person who does any unauthorised act in relation to this
publication may be liable to criminal prosecution and civil claims
for damages.

Printed in Hong Kong.

CONTENTS

	Preface	4
1	Lands of the American West	5
2	The first Americans	7
3	Plains Indians – warfare	12
4	Plains Indians – home life	14
5	White settlers move west	17
6	The California Gold Rush	20
7	The cattlemen	24
8	The life of a cowboy	29
9	The homesteaders	33
10	Billy the Kid	39
11	The Plains Wars	42
12	Battle of the Little Bighorn	47
13	The Ghost Dance and Wounded Knee	51
	Index	55
	Sources	56

Acknowledgements

The author and publishers wish to acknowledge the following photograph sources:

Denver Public Lib/Western History Dept – Western Americana Pic Lib p 19; Nebraska State Historical Society/Robert May Collection p 53; Peter Newark's Western Americana Pic Lib pp 5, 9, 10, 14, 16, 22, 24, 29, 30, 32, 34, 35, 36, 38, 39, 41, 42, 45, 48, 49, 51; Smithsonian Inst National Anthropological Archives/Western Americana Pic Lib p 52.

The publishers have made every effort to trace copyright holders, but if they have inadvertently overlooked any they will be pleased to make the necessary arrangements at the first opportunity.

PREFACE

The study of history is exciting, whether in a good story well told, a mystery solved by the judicious unravelling of clues, or a study of the men, women and children, whose fears and ambitions, successes and tragedies make up the collective memory of mankind.

This series aims to reveal this excitement to pupils through a set of topic books on important historical subjects from the Middle Ages to the present day. Each book contains four main elements: a narrative and descriptive text, lively and relevant illustrations, extracts of contemporary evidence, and questions for further thought and work. Involvement in these elements should provide an adventure which will bring the past to life in the imagination of the pupil.

Each book is also designed to develop the knowledge, skills and concepts so essential to a pupil's growth. It provides a wide, varying introduction to the evidence available on each topic. In handling this evidence, pupils will increase their understanding of basic historical concepts like causation and change, as well as of more advanced ideas like revolution and democracy. In addition, their use of basic study skills will be complemented by more sophisticated historical skills such as the detection of bias and the formulation of opinion.

The intended audience for the series is pupils of eleven to sixteen years: it is expected that the earlier topics will be introduced in the first three years of secondary school, while the nineteenth and twentieth century topics are directed towards first examinations.

Note

Much of the information we have about historical times comes from newspapers, letters, diaries and books written by men and women who knew the people and places they wrote about. These are called primary sources of information.

In this book the primary sources include the memories and observations of old people, written down or told to their children; these tell us about the changes imposed on the Indians' way of life. We can also find out about the Indians from their weapons, clothes and other objects and from the writings and paintings of white people who visited them. All these are primary sources.

Historians put all these primary sources of information together when they write their historical accounts. These modern commentaries are then called secondary sources. This book will draw on both the primary and the secondary sources of American history, and you should be able to distinguish between them.

1 LANDS OF THE AMERICAN WEST

The Sioux chief Big Foot was one of the many killed at Wounded Knee. Here his frozen body lies in the snow

The decline of the Indians

Before the arrival of the white man, one million Indians were scattered over all of North America

By 1850 the Indians had been pushed into the western half of the country

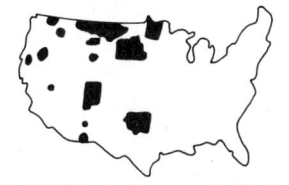

By 1875 the Indians were limited to 14 main reservations (land specially set aside for them)

The date was 29 December 1890; the place an Indian camp at Wounded Knee in South Dakota; the Indians involved, 120 adult males and 230 women and children led by the Sioux chief, Big Foot.

Big Foot and his followers had left the reservation, an area of land set aside for use by the Indians but within the borders of which they were supposed to stay. They had been caught and surrounded by 500 soldiers who ordered them to surrender their weapons. The Indians gave up only two of their rifles and the men were forced to sit in the snow in a semi-circle while soldiers searched the women for weapons. One of the medicine men tried to stir the men up against the soldiers and some of the Indians took guns from under their blankets and fired at the soldiers who fired back. Within seconds four Hotchkiss rapid-firing guns were pouring two-pound explosive shells into the Indian camp, which burst into flames; more than half of the Indians died in the first blast of fire. The surviving Indians fought fiercely, those without guns using clubs and knives. Pursued by soldiers some Indians managed to cover several miles before being overtaken and clubbed or shot to death.

Within minutes over 100 Indian men, women and children had been killed, compared to 29 dead soldiers. Three days later the frozen bodies of the Indian dead were buried naked in a long pit.

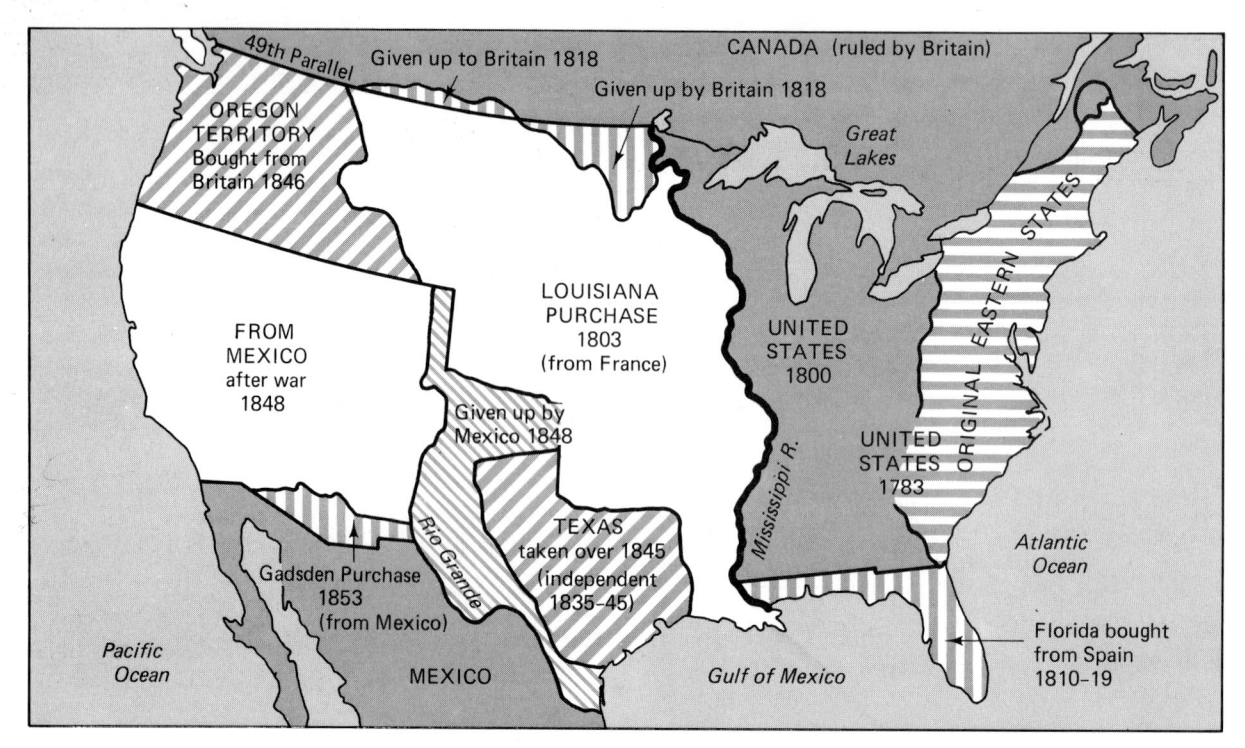

The growth of the United States 1776–1853
1. The original 13 eastern states were settled by people of mainly English, Scots, Irish and Welsh descent. In 1776 the 13 states started a successful war against their British rulers, and became known as the United States of America
2. By 1800 settlers in search of cheap land had reached the Mississippi
3. In 1803 the French, needing money for their European war, sold Louisiana to the USA for 15 million dollars. Lewis and Clark explored the Louisiana Purchase and went on to the Pacific coast. Their journals, published in 1814, inspired thousands of Americans to move further west in search of a new life
4. Spain gradually lost her land in Florida, 1810–19
5. Britain settled her argument with the USA by straightening the 49th parallel in 1818 and by transferring Oregon to America in 1846
6. Until the mid-1830s Texas had been part of Mexico, but in 1835–6 American settlers there fought for and won their freedom. Ten years passed before Texas joined the United States; in the meantime Texans were citizens of the 'Lone Star Republic'

In 1800 what was called the United States of America lay only to the east of the Mississippi River. But as new territories were occupied farther and farther west towards the Pacific Ocean so the Indians were driven westwards too. The tragedy at Wounded Knee marked the end of the struggle between the white people and the Indians.

The story of this struggle, and how the lands east of the Mississippi were conquered, developed and tamed during the nineteenth century, is the story of the American West.

2 THE FIRST AMERICANS

The arrival of the Indians

The Red Indians were the first true Americans. Their ancestors reached the Americas about 30 000 years ago, via the Bering Strait, then a virtual land-bridge – probably to escape from an ice-bound Siberia. It is estimated that about a million Indians were living in what is now the United States when white people first reached the continent.

They received the name Indians because Christopher Columbus, who landed in 1492, thought he had discovered India and called all the people then living in America 'Indians'. The word 'red' that sometimes goes before 'Indian' refers to their use of red (war or ceremonial) paint and not to their skin colour which can vary from yellow to almost black.

The arrival and spread of the Indians
1. Flatheads, Nez Percés
2. Hurons, Iroquois
3. Shawnees, Cherokees, Creeks, Seminoles, Choctaws
4. (Shaded area) Plains Indians e.g. Comanche, Kiowa, Cheyenne, Arapaho, Sioux, Blackfeet, Pawnees
5. Apaches

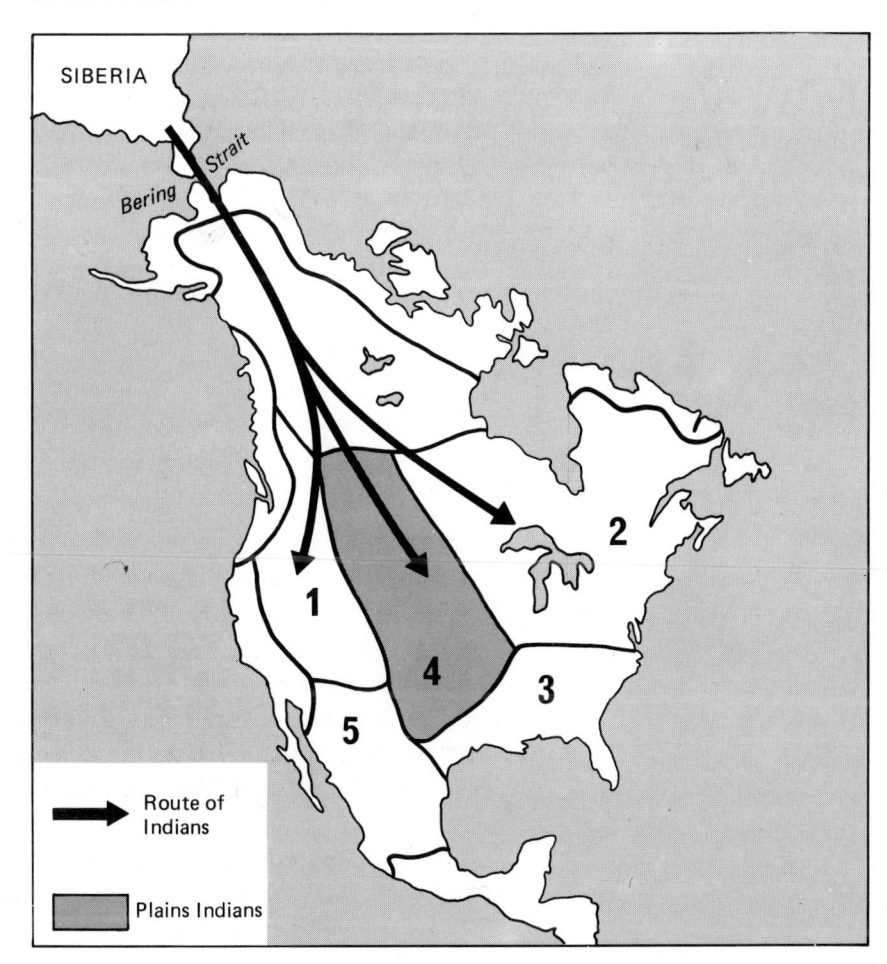

The Indian tribes

Over 300 separate groups or tribes of Indians lived in North America. Each tribe lived in a way that fitted the geography, climate and vegetation of its own area. So, for example, the forest Indian lived a different life from the prairie Indian. To show this point more clearly we shall look at the lives of the Iroquois, a forest people, and the Teton Sioux from the prairies.

(a) The Iroquois

Farming, hunting and fishing were the main activities of the Iroquois:

> *Maize, squashes and beans were the main crops. Skilled with bows and arrows, spears and slings, and at making snares, traps and pits, they hunted deer, bears, rabbits, beavers, ducks and turkeys. Animals and fish provided the Iroquois with materials for their clothes and some of their tools and weapons.*
>
> *The shoulder-blades of deer made satisfactory hoes. Bowstrings were made from the skins of turtles' necks or the sinews of deers' legs. Beaver teeth, which were long, sharp and strong, made good blades for hand-knives.*
>
> *The Iroquois made considerable use of wood. Their best bows were cut from hickory. Elm was of (first) importance in village-making and house-building. A village was usually encircled by a stockade made of elm logs. Inside were several large rectangular wooden huts with barrel-shaped roofs. These homes were called longhouses. They consisted of a framework of elm saplings covered by sheets of elm bark. A dozen families or more lived in each longhouse.* (1)

(b) The Teton Sioux

The Teton Sioux were hunters. Gathering fruit and berries, fishing and trading were minor activities. They never grew crops. It was the buffalo they were interested in and their very existence depended upon the animal:

> *The Indian women butchered the buffalo and they wasted nothing; every part of the animal was put to good use. Even the dung was dried for fuel. The liver, kidneys, brain, bone marrow and the soft nose gristle were eaten raw and considered particular delicacies.*
>
> *The hide of the buffalo was put to the greatest number of uses ... for shields and moccasin soles ... for tepee coverings, and ... for a variety of clothing. The horns and hoofs were fashioned into bowls, cups ... the shoulder blades were turned into hoes, the hair was woven into rope ... the sinews made bowstrings or thread, the fat became soap, the tail turned into a fly brush, the bones made knives and necklaces, dice and paintbrushes. Even the rough side of the tongue could be used – as a hairbrush.* (2)

Hunting Buffalo. The drawing is by George Catlin

Below   The tepee

The Sioux usually hunted buffalo by encircling the herd, causing it to panic, and then striking with lance and arrow behind the animals' shoulder blades, piercing the heart (see chapter 3).

The Teton Sioux followed the buffalo wherever they roamed across the huge prairies, and because of this roving life they needed moveable homes. They lived in tepees (left). The tepee was made of three poles lashed together, covered with buffalo skins and was easy to put up and take down, very weatherproof, roomy, warm in winter and cool in summer. It housed one family.

Questions
1. Make a list of the ways in which the Iroquois life differed from that of the Sioux. Use the following headings: the sort of food they ate; the ways of finding food; types of housing.
2. Can you think of any reasons for the differences you have listed?

tepee

settlement or town

horse rider

trade or exchange

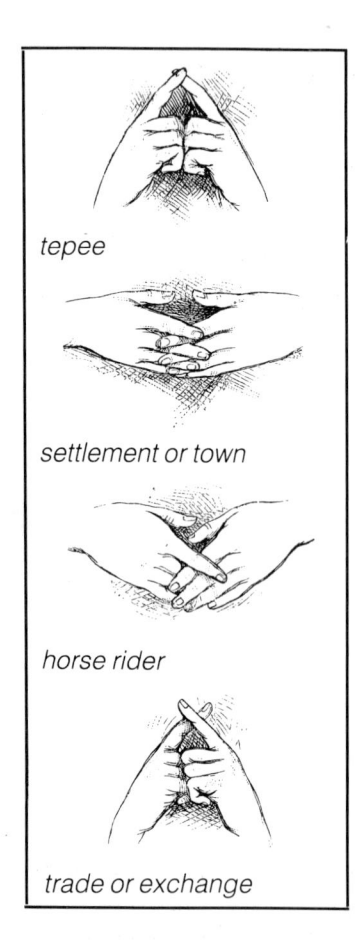

Sign language

Kinship: close relationship

Sign language

Tribes often had different languages, so how did they understand each other? The answer is by a form of hand sign-language which was understood by all the tribes on the Great Plains and, in many cases, beyond them.

Assignment
In pairs practise the hand signals shown here. Invent for yourself other signs that would be useful for Indians. Perhaps you could start with: eat, false (forked tongue), alone. Then think of your own signs. Try to pass messages by these signs to your partner. Afterwards discuss the disadvantages of sign language.

The beliefs that the Indian tribes had in common

Although there were many differences between tribes, they did have important beliefs in common. All Indians felt very close to nature. All creatures were their brothers, even those they had to hunt. They loved the land and the earth, believing that it belonged to all people, animals and plants. One Sioux chief, Luther Standing Bear, wrote:

The Sioux was a true lover of nature. He loved the earth and all things of the earth. Their tepees were built upon the earth. The birds that flew in the air came to rest upon the earth and it was the final abiding-place of all things that lived and grew ... Kinship with all creatures of the earth, sky and water was a real and active (belief) ... (3)

Indians were religious, believing in 'medicine' – the spirit that protected them in everyday life and in battle. All Indians loved freedom, so much so that even their chiefs could only advise, not order, the warriors of the tribe. The belief in freedom meant that even if on the battlefield:

a brave broke off the fight to go hunt an antelope ... he had no fear that he would be accused of being a coward on his return to the village. (4)

The Indians' attitude to the land
The Indians developed a special feeling for their land and the earth. The idea that anyone could buy or sell land was strange to them.

The difference between the Indians' attitude to the land and the white people's is examined in the chart below:

The Indians' view	The white people's view
No tribe has the right to sell (land), even to each other, much less to strangers. Sell a country! Why not sell the air, the great sea, as well as the earth (5) *Our land is more valuable than your money. It will not even perish by the flames of fire. As long as the sun shines, and the waters flow, this land will be here to give life to men and animals. We cannot sell the lives of men and animals, therefore, we cannot sell this land. It was put here for us by the Great Spirit and we cannot sell it because it does not belong to us.* A Blackfoot Chief (7)	*The land is 'property to be bought ... mined, grazed or lived on'* (6)
My father sent for me. I saw he was dying. He said 'My son, my body is returning to my mother earth... This country holds your father's body. Never sell the bones of your father and your mother.' My father smiled and passed away... I buried him in that beautiful valley of winding waters. I loved that land more than all the rest of the world. A man who would not love his father's grave is worse than a wild animal. Chief Joseph of the Nez Percé's tribe (8)	*The average Indian of the prairies is a being who does little credit to human nature. As I passed over ... the very best cornlands on earth and saw their owners sitting around the doors of their lodges at the height of the planting season I could not help saying, 'These people must die out — there is no help for them. God has given this earth to those who will (tame) and cultivate it.'* Horace Greeley (9)

Great Spirit: God

cultivate: to grow crops

Exercise

Imagine you are a Sioux Indian, and you are having a conversation with a white man. The white man has started off by saying: 'I cannot understand you Indians. You must be really lazy. Why don't you settle down in one place, plough up the earth and start growing some crops? If you don't want to do this, sell the land to me.' Now reply to the white man.

3 PLAINS INDIANS~WARFARE

The coming of the horse

The Indians of the plains were nomadic, so when the buffalo moved to new grazing grounds, the Indians moved with them (see chapter 2). Until 1700 they followed the buffalo on foot since they did not have horses. In 1540 the Spaniards had brought horses to America, but would not sell any to the Indians. However, in 1680 the Pueblo Indians rose against the Spanish, drove them out and captured their horse herds. Over the next few years the horse spread to the plains and produced an amazing change of lifestyle for the various tribes that lived in that area (see map on page 7):

> ... to the Plains Indians ... the horse meant power and freedom... Horse trading became an Indian profession; wealth was calculated by the number of horses a man possessed. Instead of a trudging foot-people confined to the fringe of the prairies, the Plains Indians quickly became the finest riders in the world.
> In a sudden blaze of mobility they poured out on to the plains. Farming was forgotten. On horseback they could travel vast distances. With these wonderful beasts they could carry all their belongings easily, and kill more buffalo than they had ever dreamed possible. Comanche, Kiowa, Cheyenne, Arapahoe, Sioux, Nez Percé, Blackfoot ... soon the plains were divided among these mobile, warrior tribes.' (1)

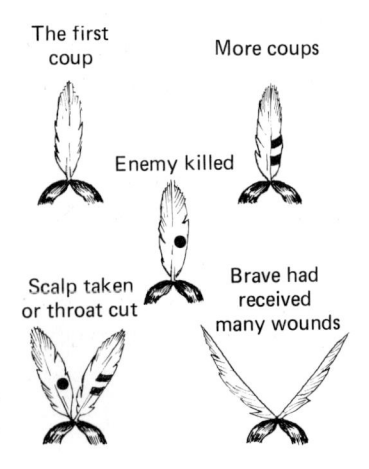

The first coup
More coups
Enemy killed
Scalp taken or throat cut
Brave had received many wounds

Eagle feathers were given as a sign of brave deeds

Question
In what ways did the horse change the Indians' way of life?

The importance of bravery

To gain the love of a woman, become a chief, or earn respect, could only be achieved by bravery in battle as this Sioux love song shows:

> *You may go on the warpath*
> *When your name I hear,*
> *Having done something brave*
> *Then I will marry you.* (2)

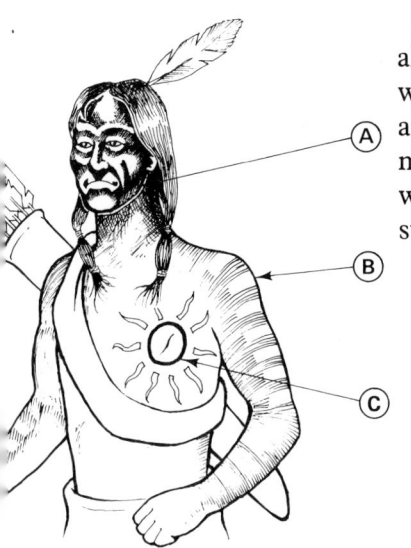

A blackened face shows that the fires of his revenge are burned out
B 'coup' marks
C a wound encircled with healing rays of the sun

A Sioux warrior back from a raid. The bravest deed was not to kill your enemy but to count 'coup' – that is, the touching or striking of an enemy with the hand or a special stick, during the fight

To the Indian it was important to show bravery and then get back alive. Since he was the hunter and provider for his family his death would bring hardship. Because of their skill and speed as horsemen and archers, the Indians' tactic in battle was to attack swiftly and then make a rapid retreat. They were very good at 'hit and run' warfare which involved the use of small bands of warriors, ambushes and sudden attacks. White men thought these tactics were cowardly:

Indians fight in a way very different to civilised people; for they depend more on cunning ... and surprise, than on skill and courage. Almost all their attacks are made under cover of night, or when least expected.... They will hide for any length of time in the forest, sleep in the long grass, lurk in the ravine, and skulk at nightfall around the place to be attacked. (3)

Questions
1 In extract (3) does the writer approve or disapprove of Indian war tactics? Find any words or phrases which make his attitude clear.
2 Do you think the Indians fought like cowards or that they made the best possible use of their knowledge, skill and weapons? Explain your answer.
3 Why do you think some braves were prepared to ride into battle unarmed?

Most Indian battles were to capture horses from other tribes. The Plains Indians rarely made war with the main aim of killing their enemy or torturing prisoners. There was scalping and torture, but with the exception of the Comanche most Plains Indians regarded warfare as a sport. According to one modern historian, Indian warfare:

... was almost a pastime, a sport, a game that could be called off if it ... became too rough. Deaths were kept to a minimum and captives were normally well treated. (4)

However, when the white invaders began to threaten the very existence of the Indian, the 'game' of war turned into a bitter struggle for survival. Cruelty and terror then became common on both sides.

4 PLAINS INDIANS – HOME LIFE

Childhood

The Indians loved their children very much. They never punished them, except in extreme cases when they threw a bowl of cold water over them. Indian children were never beaten or screamed at. They were asked to do something, not told.

There was no formal school, no learning to read or write, but simply instruction by the older members of the tribe in skills necessary for adulthood. The boys were trained to:

> mount while their horses were running at full speed, running a few steps by the side of the horse, then grasping its mane and springing in the air (1)

The girls would be taught by their mothers that:

> women's work was to cook for the family, keep the tepee in order, and sew the clothing of the household members. (2)

Religion

Indians were very religious. They believed in spirits, which were everywhere around them – in the thunder and lightning, the trees, streams and animals. It was important to please these spirits. The Medicine Man was therefore very important since it was believed he could talk to the spirits, learn their thoughts and feelings and even persuade them to do what he asked. Medicine Men were also expected to see into the future and heal the sick.

The most important tribal ceremony of the year was the Sun Dance during which braves thrust skewers through their chests and attached them by long strings to the top of a large pole. Then they danced around the pole, praying and looking towards the sun all the time. The dance ended when the flesh was ripped away from the chest and the skewer and its strings fell to the floor. This dance showed the warriors' bravery. It also brought dreams or visions by which the dancer could contact the spirits and bring good fortune.

Part of the Sun Dance *by Frederic Remington*

Old people

Old people were treated with great respect. They were thought to be very wise. Grandmothers played an important part in rearing young children. Great care was taken to provide food for the old and sick. Black Elk described the scene just before a buffalo hunt:

> ... *the best hunters with the fastest horses, were told: 'Young warriors, your work I know is good; so today you shall feed the helpless. Perhaps there are some old and feeble people without sons, or some who have little children and no man. You shall help these and whatever you kill shall be theirs'. This was a great honour for young men.* (3)

Being generous was of great importance to the Indian. It ranked higher than bravery or hunting skill. An Indians' happiness was to give; to provide for the helpless ones. Yet the Sioux were always on the move following the buffalo and because of this the old and weak, if unable to ride or walk, were left behind. The white people found this custom very difficult to understand.

Question
The white people thought that the Indians were very cruel people. Do you think the Indians' treatment of the young and the elderly show this opinion to be true or false? Explain your answer.

Government

The tribes of the Plains Indians divided into small groups or bands to search for food. The Cheyenne tribe split into ten bands, each of which had between three and five hundred people and was governed by a council of elders who would meet with the chief to discuss important matters and make decisions. Any man who had ability could be chosen as chief. The chiefs did not give orders, they merely offered advice. The bands of a tribe did not act together. This might mean that some would be at peace while others were on the warpath.

The hunters and warriors of the Cheyenne tribe were called 'dog soldiers' and acted as a police force:

encampments: the place where the Indian camps were set up
designate: choose

> *It is they who protect and supply the women and children. From them come all orders for marches. By them the encampments are selected. They supply the guards for the camp and designate the hunting parties.* (4)

If an Indian was guilty of a serious crime he could be turned out of the tribe and left to look after himself. In some cases the offender would have to give presents to his victim's family.

A Sioux horse race. Archery, wrestling and gambling were other popular Indian pastimes

Questions

1. What difficulties might face the United States government if it wished to make a treaty with the Cheyenne tribe?
2. The plains Indians never had prisons:
   (a) What was there about the Teton Siouxs' way of life which meant it was unlikely that they could keep long-term prisoners?
   (b) One Indian chief said that he would rather be tortured than imprisoned. Why did the Indians think that putting someone in prison was very cruel? Think of the Indian beliefs that you read about in chapter 2.

5 WHITE SETTLERS MOVE WEST

The town of Independence, Missouri, stood at the start of three trails or routes followed by the wagon trains. In the wagons came settlers looking for a new home and a new life.

Why go west?

Some went west for religious reasons. The Mormons, a religious group, simply wanted to find a place where they could worship and live in their own way. Brigham Young led his people to the Salt Lake Valley of Utah, where the Mormons built Salt Lake City.

But mostly it was farmers who went west. They were attracted by stories of rich fertile soil and buyers who would pay high prices for their crops.

Newspapermen and politicians were anxious to make even the most exaggerated reports of conditions in Oregon and California widely known. If settlers believed the reports they would crowd into the areas. Oregon could then be won by the Americans from the British who also claimed the area. Similarly, California could be taken from the Mexicans.

Dangers and difficulties on the trail

In spite of what films and television suggest, Indians were by no means the greatest danger on the trail. Indians never attacked a wagon train in the 1840s on the Oregon trail. The attacks came later, in the 1860s, after the white people had stolen Indian land, and massacres had led to hatred on both sides. Far more common than attacks by Indians were the everyday hazards of accident and disease:

> *At least 20 000, about one of every 17 who started, were buried along the Oregon trail. Along some stretches of the route graves were so numerous that the trail developed a saw-tooth edge – a border of footpaths worn by the curious going off to the side to read the wooden grave markers.* (1)

The California trail was the toughest of them all but the promise of land of their own meant that many people were willing to risk their lives for a 'new start'.

Wagon trails west

The mountain passes were the steepest in the world. Sometimes ten or more oxen were needed to pull one wagon up a slope, while men pushed from behind. Ropes were needed to lower the wagons down the other side of the slope. The mountains could only be crossed when free from snow and because of this wagon trains started out from Missouri before the end of May so as to get to the Sierra Mountains well before the snow started to fall. However, one wagon train, the Donner party, started out late and then took an untested 'shortcut' which in fact delayed them by nearly two months.

the party was caught by ... early snowfalls in the California Sierras ... and forced to camp there until rescue parties could arrive ... Food ran out and some members of the party managed to (live) on the hides of their dead cattle, which at first they had used to roof their tents ... Others resorted to cannibalism, to some extent at least, though it has never been proved that any member of the party was actually killed in order to be eaten. Enough anyway, died of starvation and exhaustion. (2)

In Sioux Indian country. Careful watch kept. Indians did not often attack wagon trains. They hardly ever attacked when the wagons were drawn up in a circle, since, as one historian has written:

The Indian was a sensible fellow, not wishing more than anyone else to get himself killed. Why should he go galloping around in that silly and hopeless fashion exposing himself and his pony to rifle fire from men in a sheltered position? (4)

Shoshoni Indian country. Indians not warlike but they are thieves. Heat makes everyone weary and tired.

Fort Hall was reached during August

Sioux war parties sometimes spotted

South Pass through the Rockies

Fort Laramie reached by the end of June

Oregon City

SIERRA MOUNTAINS

Salt Lake City — Fort Bridger

Sacramento

San Francisco

Sutter's Fort. Wagons arrived by mid-October

Tough going. Desert and rough mountain country. Shortage of grass and water. Weaker oxen die

Denver
Pike's Peak

Santa Fe

Easy going. People now used to wagons and enjoying themselves

Independence (Missouri)
St Joseph
Kansas City

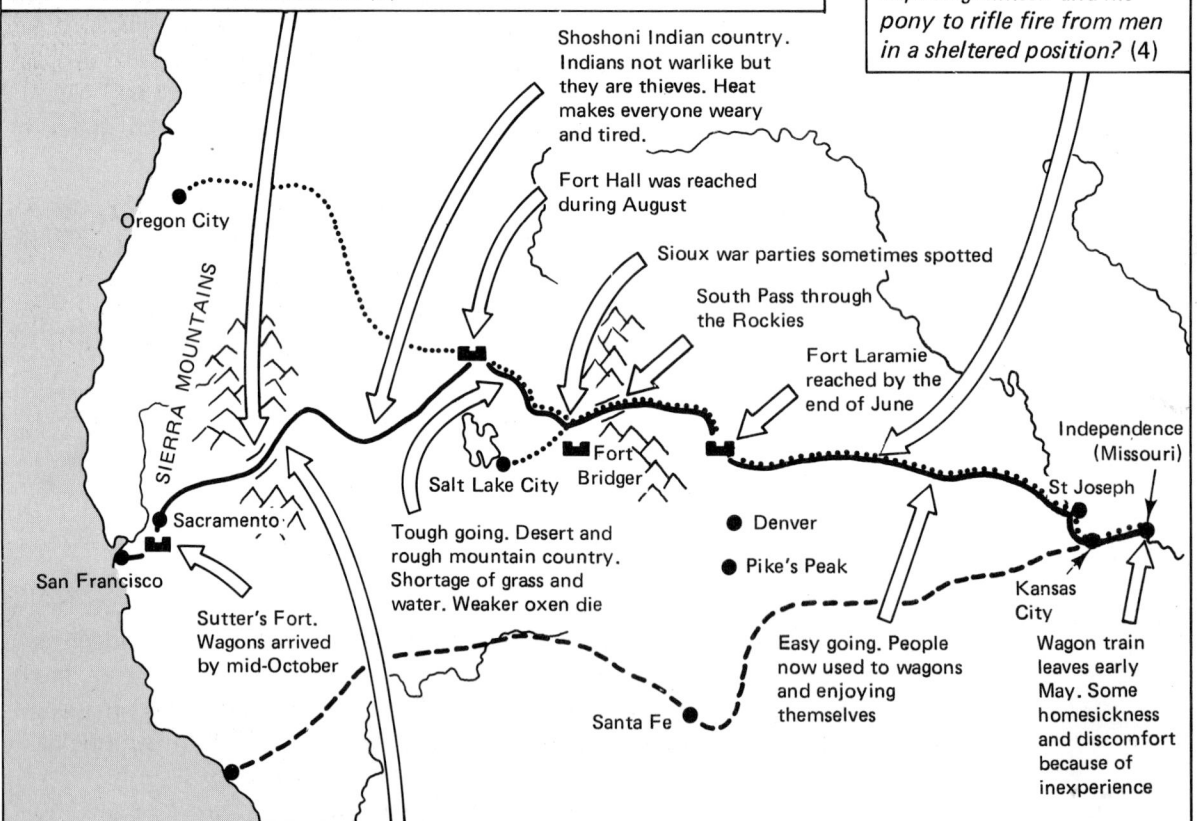

Wagon train leaves early May. Some homesickness and discomfort because of inexperience

The 55-mile wide Humboldt Desert. No water was available.
They could make it in fifty-two hours. But the parched animals were used to a rest at the 'nooning'. They couldn't let them. They had to push on, and when the animals collapsed they left them to die. One man wrote later that you could not possibly mistake the trail because it was littered at intervals of only thirty yards or so with rusting shafts ... skeletons of mules and oxen and the corpses of humans. Some people died of starvation, of thirst ... They crossed sticks and laid them over the body: 'Tom Walmsley, born Yorkshire, died this spot, August 10 1849 (3)

Whole families went west in search of a new life. The canvas-covered wagon measured about four metres long by one metre. Horses were too expensive and too weak for hauling wagons and so were kept for saddle riding. The real choice lay between mules and oxen with the latter generally preferred because they were very cheap. The wagons covered about 16–19 km (10–12 miles) per day. For many the journey must have seemed very uncomfortable and never ending

Questions
1. Imagine that you have to produce a programme for radio about the wagon-trains on the California Trail: make a list of the features of the journey that you would mention and write a scene to illustrate each of them. Then write a commentary. You may wish to tape-record this material and try adding sound effects.
2. What qualities of character would the travellers on the wagon-train have needed?
3. What made the journey west worthwhile?

The results of the westward movement

By 1845, 6 000 Americans lived in Oregon (and many more were to follow) compared with only 750 British settlers. Within a year the British government had agreed to give up its claim to Oregon.

In California, as the number of Americans grew, quarrels with the Mexicans increased. In the end a war between the United States and Mexico broke out. The Mexicans were defeated and agreed to give up California (see page 6).

Question
How do you think the wagon-trains contributed to the settlement of the United States?

6 THE CALIFORNIA GOLD RUSH

On 24 January 1848, James Marshall and John Sutter discovered gold at Sutter's Creek in the Sacramento valley of California. As other finds were made, 'gold fever' spread over California.

The way to the gold

Soon news of the gold had spread around the world. Fortune-seekers made hurried preparations to get to California. There were three main routes:
1. overland across the Plains and the Rocky Mountains
2. across the Isthmus of Panama and by sea to California
3. the sea route round Cape Horn

The overland route

This was by far the most popular route. In addition to the usual hazards on the California Trail (see chapter 5) the killer disease called cholera was particularly widespread. A journalist described the miners' difficulties:

> The cholera ... overtook them before they were fairly embarked on the wilderness ... Men were seized without warning with the most violent symptoms ... sufferers were (sometimes) left to die by the roadside, while their panic-stricken companions pushed forwards, vainly trusting to get beyond the influence of the cholera ... Many, who in their anxiety to get forward with speed, had thrown away supplies, now began to want, and were frequently reduced to making use of their mules and horses for food. It was not unusual to kill a quantity of rattlesnakes and have a dish of them, fried, for supper. (1)

However, the route did have advantages. It was fairly short – about 16 000 km (approximately 10 000 miles), shorter, for example, than the trip round the Horn. It was also cheaper, since the average traveller by sea routes needed at least 300 dollars to start. Many Americans, especially if they were farmers, also already owned much of what they needed for the overland trip, e.g. wagons, oxen and food.

The Panama route

Rather than go all the way around Cape Horn, many thought it would be a good idea to take a 'short-cut' across the Isthmus of Panama to the Pacific coastline, and wait for a ship to take them to San Francisco. However, the five-day journey across the Isthmus was tough and

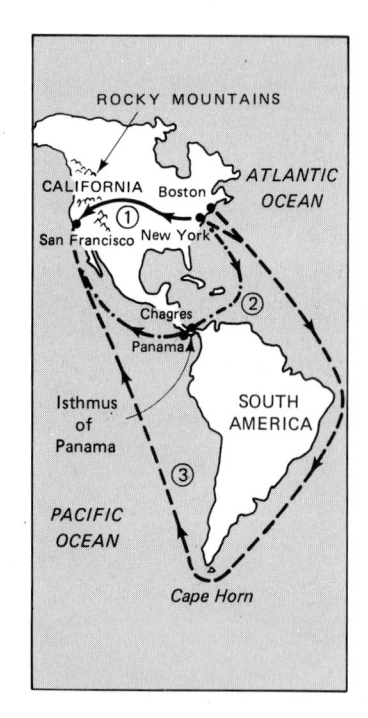

The routes to California

dangerous – swamps, jungles and killer diseases. Also, once at Panama, the traveller usually had a long wait for a ship and plenty of competition for a limited number of places aboard:

> *When the steamer put in at Panama City ... she was greeted by fifteen hundred men camped on the beach in a miserable, disease-ridden, unsanitary scramble of tents and hutches. Riot threatened until finally the Captain stuffed four hundred men aboard a vessel built for two hundred. Passengers slept on the deck, the water was rationed, provisions ran so low that the steward took on a stock of monkeys...* (2)

Question
Why do you think this route might prove to be more expensive than you first thought?

Round the Horn
This was a slow route taking six to eight months. It was, however, the safest. Seasickness and boredom were major problems. The ocean route did have advantages though – large amounts of baggage and equipment could be taken along and, unlike the overland traveller whose movements were governed by the seasons, the Cape voyagers could leave at almost any time.

Question
Considering points such as cost and safety, say which route you would take if:
(a) you were poor and single;
(b) you were married and wished to take your family with you.
Give reasons for your answers and in each case say why you rejected the other routes.

Life in the Californian gold fields

Very few miners struck it lucky and earned a fortune. The majority earned about 100 dollars a month in 1849 and 50 dollars in 1852. Some were not so fortunate:

> *One, after three months of toil, found that he had cleared only one penny a day; another averaged three dollars daily after work that would have killed a horse.* (3)

Panning for gold by sifting sand and sediment from the river bed. Gold was often found in rivers where it had been washed down from the gold-ore deposits in the hills. The gold which could be mined easily was soon gone. It then became necessary to use machinery to crush rock or direct jets of water into hillsides to bring away gold-bearing material

1 gallon = 4.5. litres
100 cents = 1 dollar
1 lb = 0.45 kg

Food and materials were very expensive to buy:

Food and materials	Cost of items
Eggs	5 dollars for 10
Milk	2 dollars a gallon
Bread	75 cents a loaf
Potatoes	1 dollar per 1b
Tea and coffee	1 dollar per 1b
Barrel of flour	100 dollars
Shovel	10 dollars
Work Shirt	16 dollars

Questions

1. Why do you think many miners were earning less in 1852 than in 1849?
2. Who do you think really got rich in California?
3. Look carefully at the picture above. What can it tell us about the living and working conditions of the miners?

The miner's diet lacked vegetables. It consisted mainly of bread, coffee and pork. 'I've lived on swine till I grunt and squeal', went one of the miner's songs. On this diet he had to work long hours in cold streams beneath a scorching sun. His clothes, blue denim overalls

(Levis), woollen shirts (red, blue or striped) were rarely changed because laundresses charged eight dollars to wash a dozen shirts. Some miners even found it cheaper to send their dirty clothes to China to be laundered!

The importance of the miners

California's population increased tremendously as compared with other states during this period:

Year	California	Oregon	Utah
1848	14 000	12 000	
1850	100 000		11 000
1852	250 000		
1860	380 000	52 000	40 000

Without the discovery of gold, California would probably have remained under-populated for decades, separated as it was from the settled eastern states by a thousand miles of open and often inhospitable country. The settlement of California meant that the land between California and the Mississippi – 'The Great American Desert' as some Americans called it – was developing more speedily than would otherwise have been the case.

Gold and silver were discovered in other areas: in Colorado (1838), Idaho (1840), Montana (1862), Arizona (1863) and the Black Hills of Dakota (1874). These discoveries were very important for the settlement of the West:

> *Wherever gold was discovered, not only mines but also mining camps grew up. In time many became thriving towns such as Virginia City and Denver. The miners needed food and ... goods and so cattlemen, traders and other people were soon attracted to the region. The demands of the mining areas for improved transportation also spurred on the building of a transcontinental railway (i.e. one that would link the eastern and western seaboards).* (4)

The completion of the transcontinental railroad (1869) attracted the attention of the cattlemen (chapter 7) and led to the growth of cattle towns like Abilene and Dodge City. The railways brought settlers to the prairies and supplied them with not only food and clothing but with machinery needed to tame the land. The markets for the farmers were in the East and Europe. The farmers link with these places was the railroad.

7 THE CATTLEMEN

The first white people on the Great Plains

The Great Plains covered a huge and remote area.

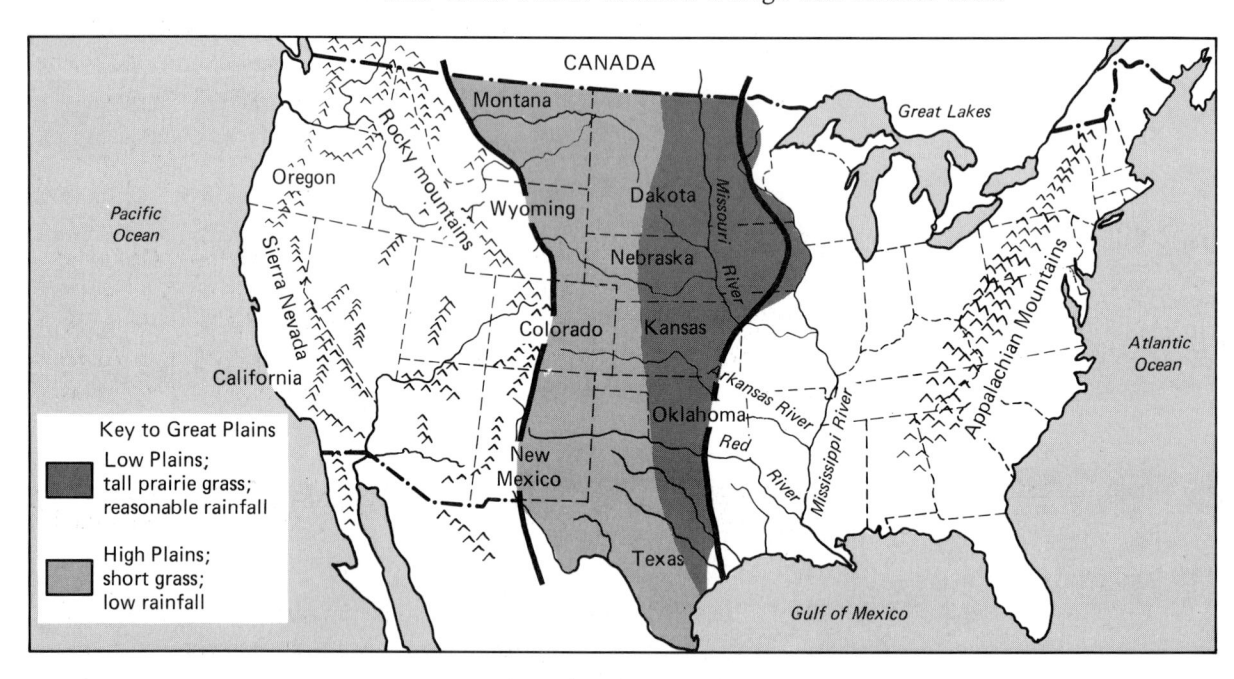

The Great Plains in relation to the rest of the United States

Texas Longhorn cattle

Much of it was windswept and treeless, scorching in summer and freezing in winter. Until the 1850s it was called a desert and a traveller would have seen a vast landscape with little but buffalo and sky, wild game and Indians. By 1890 this had changed. The cattlemen and cowboys were to show that it was no desert, and their success in the region was to encourage farmers to follow and settle in the area.

Question
Why were the plains regarded as unsuitable for farming?

The Cattle Kingdom

The Texas cattle industry began in the 1830s, at the time when Texas was breaking away from Mexico (see chapter 1, page 6). The Texans laid claim to all the cattle the Mexicans had left behind. The cattle were mostly longhorns, noted for their tremendous horns which sometimes measured 2 metres from tip to tip.

The Texans started ranching, and drove herds to places such as New Orleans and California. After the Civil War (the war between the northern and southern states of America 1861–5) the defeated Texans returned home to find most of their ranches run down and hundreds of thousands of longhorns running wild. During the winter of 1865–6 the Texans were hard at work, rounding up the cattle and hiring cowboys to drive the cattle north where, because of a shortage of beef, cattle were sold for as much as 30–40 dollars a head. Most cattlemen drove their herds north-east to Sedalia where the railway would then take the cattle eastwards. It proved to be a far from easy business:

Heavy rains muddied the ground. Beyond the Red River, Indians stampeded the herds and then demanded a reward for returning the longhorns to their owners...

Farther on, angry farmers came out, fearing that the cattle would trample down their crops and shooting the leaders when they failed to stop. To make matters worse, bands of outlaws (they were called 'jayhawkers' or 'redlegs' after the red strip down the military trousers that many still wore) turned on the cowboys and attempted to rob the herds. (1)

Joseph M. McCoy, a cattle dealer, realising these difficulties, decided a safer spot to aim for would be Abilene on the Kansas Pacific Railroad. He wrote:

Abilene was selected because the country was entirely unsettled, well watered, had excellent grass, and nearly the entire area of country was adapted to holding cattle. (2)

35 000 cattle reached Abilene in 1867. The figures for the next four years are shown below:

Year	No. of cattle
1868	75 000
1869	350 000
1870	300 000
1871	700 000

Question
What were the motives of the various groups hindering the cattle from reaching Sedalia?

As the railway line was built further west more 'cow towns' were set up, such as Dodge City, Ellsworth and Wichita. New trails were laid

The cattle trails

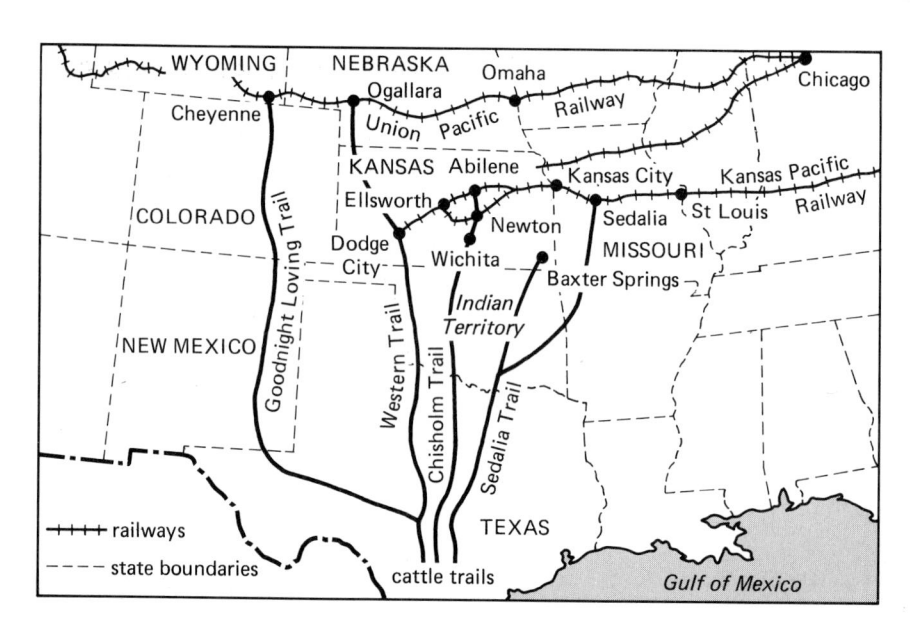

heading for these towns. Each in its turn had its day and became the centre of trade.

Opposition to the cattlemen

Soon the cattlemen were to face opposition. The railway across the prairies brought not only the cattlemen but settlers too. As the settlers moved west their farms increasingly blocked the cattle trails. Teddy 'Blue' Abbot, a cowboy, complained:

cussing: swearing

> [They] ... would take up a claim right where the herds watered and charge us for water. They would plant a crop alongside the trail and plow a furrow around it for a fence, and then when the cattle got into their wheat or their garden patch, they would come out cussing and waving a shotgun and yelling for damages. (3)

There were other problems too:

> The Indians ... who had been granted land on the prairie by the Government, began to charge the cowboys a toll of 10 cents a head to bring the longhorns across their reservations. (4)

The cattlemen therefore decided that if they could no longer drive their cattle north from the old breeding grounds in Texas, then they must breed their cattle out on the prairie close to the railroads.

Question
Why do you think cattle ranching spread outside Texas between 1865 and 1880?

The ranch and the open range

The open range was the unfenced land on which the cattle grazed. No one owned this land and it was supposed to be free for all to use.

Ranch houses (where the cattlemen and cowboys lived) were built, and around the ranch house the cattle grazed on the open range. Some ranchers took over vast acres of land and filled them with as many as 150 000 head of cattle. By 1885 no more than thirty-five men controlled over eight million hectares of range, and owned at least a third of all the cattle on the prairies. If farmers dared to move on to this free land the 'cattle barons' (big cattle ranchers) would use force to get rid of them. Soon cattle ranching had spread all over the Great Plains.

The end of the open range

Until 1885 everything went well for the cattlemen. Prices for beef were high, and good profits were made. Then, in 1885 things began to go wrong. Ranchers who were eager to make quick profits brought in too many cattle, which simply ate the grass faster than it could grow. The weather, too, was disastrous. A Montana rancher later explained what happened:

roundup: each year a rancher would gather and collect all of his cattle that were running loose on the range. Later they would be taken to market and sold

> *The spring roundup (of 1886) did not start until May 25, because with the continued drought the green grass would not start...*
>
> *Added to the drought was tremendous heat. The thermometer stood at 100–110°F (38–43°C) and then would come hot winds that licked up every drop of moisture and shrivelled the grass.*
>
> *December 5, there was (a) storm, with the thermometer 12°F below (−23°C) and four inches (10 cm) of snow. On the night of January 15 (the thermometer) stood at 46°F below zero (−43°C), and there were sixteen inches (40 cm) of snow on the level... Everything was white. The storm lasted ten days... and fat young steers froze to death.*
>
> *There was a series of storms in February and while not so severe yet they came at a time when the cattle were least able to withstand them and there were heavy losses...* (5)

This nightmare winter killed at least half of the cattle on the range and in some areas eighty per cent of them. It forced the ranchers to think again.

Question
Why was 1885–6 such a bad time for the cattle ranchers (read extract 5)?

The fencing of the range

Farmers objected to the free-roaming cattle which destroyed their richest crops, so they started fencing off their land with barbed wire – a new invention. The cattle barons were horrified. Furious quarrels also developed between people claiming they owned the same land and water. Conflict between cattlemen and homesteaders (farmers who set up house on the prairies) was particularly serious in Johnson County, Wyoming. The cattlemen accused the homesteaders of cattle rustling (thieving cattle) and started hanging homesteaders. Eventually troops had to be brought in to re-establish law and order.

However, after their recent disasters, the cattle barons began to see the sense of fencing. It would enable them to keep out neighbours' cattle which were eating all the grass. They could also fence off some of their own land and use it for growing hay for winter fodder. Furthermore, many ranchers were trying to improve their herds by cross-breeding. They did not want wild Texas cattle giving diseases to their better stock. Finally a second invention, the portable windpump or windmill, enabled the rancher to fence off his land even where there was no water. With the aid of the windpump he could then draw up water from underground.

Changes in the cowboy's life

Fencing brought an end to the roundup and the long drive (see chapter 8). Cowboys now had to ride along the fences, mending and repairing both the barbed wire and the windmills. Many cowboys wished they were back in the days of the roundup and cattle drive.

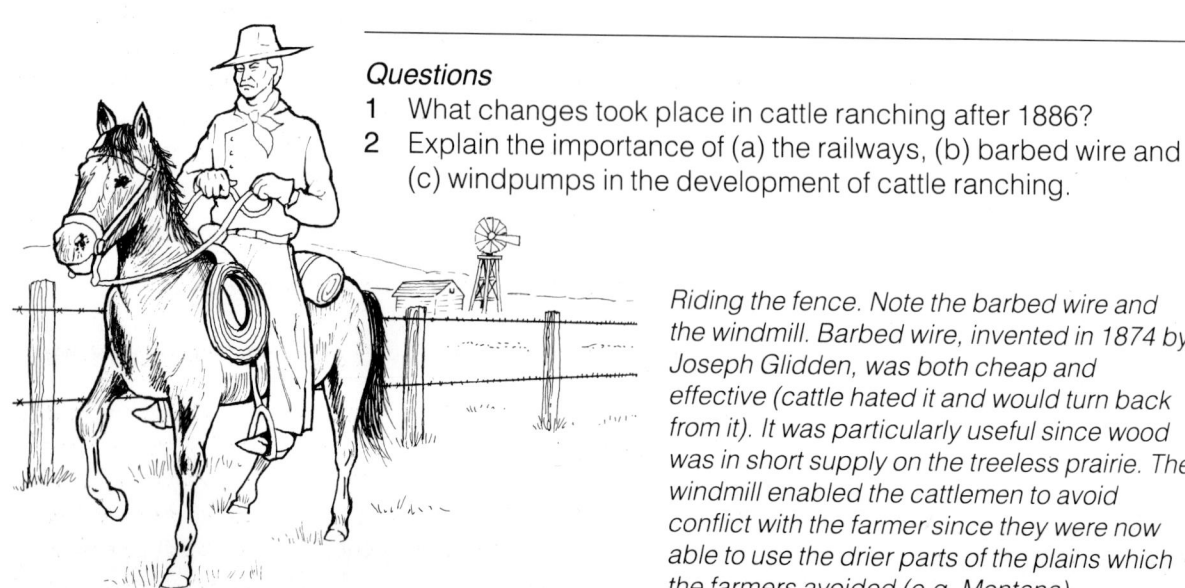

Questions
1. What changes took place in cattle ranching after 1886?
2. Explain the importance of (a) the railways, (b) barbed wire and (c) windpumps in the development of cattle ranching.

Riding the fence. Note the barbed wire and the windmill. Barbed wire, invented in 1874 by Joseph Glidden, was both cheap and effective (cattle hated it and would turn back from it). It was particularly useful since wood was in short supply on the treeless prairie. The windmill enabled the cattlemen to avoid conflict with the farmer since they were now able to use the drier parts of the plains which the farmers avoided (e.g. Montana)

8 THE LIFE OF A COWBOY

When we think of a cowboy we probably think of six-shooters, fist fights, excitement and adventure. We remember the exciting things, like riding a bucking bronco. We imagine a romantic figure complete with hat, spurs and guns, riding into the sunset on a beautiful horse.

Real cowboys had a different view of their job. One complained of 'never-ending ... weary days and sleepless nights,' and modern historians have shown that the cowboy was actually a dirty, overworked, underpaid labourer.

Questions
1. What image of the cowboy does this portrait by Remington put across?
2. A portrait is one kind of non-written historical evidence; suggest, with examples, three other types of non-written evidence that would help us find out about the life of the cowboy.
3. We have very few accounts of cowboy life written by real cowboys. Can you suggest a reason for this?

Bucking Bronco by western artist Frederic Remington. A bronco was an untamed horse

The first cowboys learned their job from the Mexican 'vaqueros' in Texas. The name means 'cow-herder' and comes from 'vaca', the Spanish word for cow. The cowboy was simply a hired hand. His job was to look after the cattle. Throughout the winter and early spring the cattle grazed on the open range under the watchful eye of the cowboy. In late spring the cattle were rounded up and branded with a mark so that they could be easily identified. In summer the cattle were taken to market (the trail drive).

The dangers and hardships of cowboy life

The following two extracts show how the cowboy had a hard life:

In the early days before fences, cow outfits employed line riders and maintained line camps 'long the borders of their range in which were quartered one or more cowboys whose duty it was to keep the cattle of their brand 'throwed back' on their own range, and to prevent 'em from driftin' in winter... Among some of the duties of the line rider was the drivin' of cattle away from patches of loco weed, or

brand: mark made on the cattle to show who owned them

(poisoned) water holes... If he ran across an animal (stuck) in a boghole he had to rope it and pull it to dry ground.

Men selected to winter in them camps were usually single men with few or no home ties... His was a lonely two meal-a-day job... (1)

The hardships of the trail included thieves, Indians and angry settlers, also floods, swollen rivers, storms, prairie fires, stampedes and falls. With such a list no wonder that cowboys recalled lack of sleep as being the worst hardship of all. No wonder that young healthy men reached the cowtowns exhausted and liable to go wild...

Cowboys were knocked from their horses by lightning and many were killed or badly burned by it. It was hardly surprising that many of them were terrified of it – and let it be remembered that they could never take shelter: their duty was towards their cattle. (2)

The stampede, which the cowboys feared the most, was terrifying:

The earth trembled under the clatter of hoofs, horns clanged and a great heat was generated ... the smell from the clashing horns and hoofs was almost overpowering. Those hands not already mounted sprang into their saddles and galloped after the herd. They could not stop them, but tried to turn them into a huge circle.

It is often stated that cowboys fired their pistols into the ground near the stampeders' ears to make them turn, but Teddy Blue, a veteran of many stampedes, claimed this was all fiction and would have made the cattle run even faster...

After the stampede there was always a danger of another – and another. One herd stampeded eighteen times in a single night. Some stampedes could be ended in four or five miles, but some went on for a week and covered hundreds of miles. (3)

A cowboy trying to stop a stampede

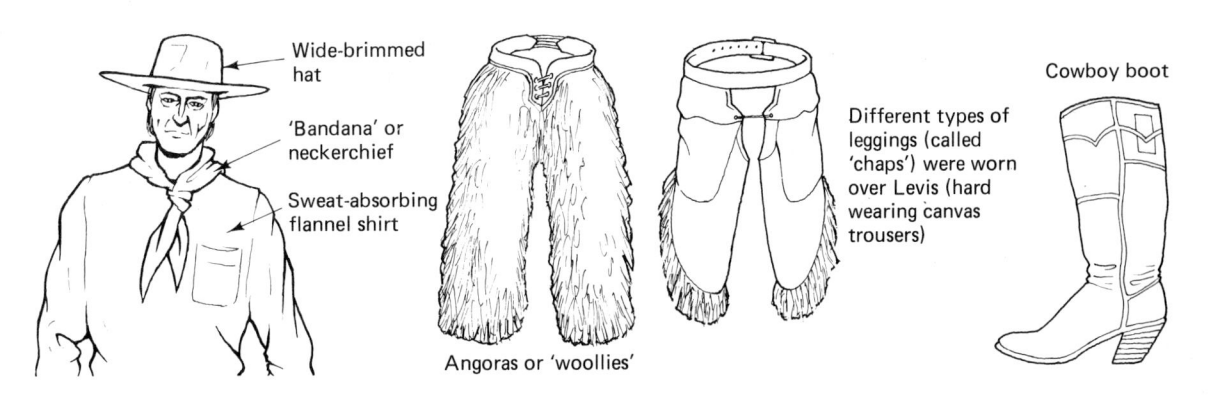

A cowboy's outfit

Labels on illustration: Wide-brimmed hat; 'Bandana' or neckerchief; Sweat-absorbing flannel shirt; Angoras or 'woollies'; Different types of leggings (called 'chaps') were worn over Levis (hard wearing canvas trousers); Cowboy boot

The other occasion when the cattle might panic was mid-stream on a river crossing. Cowboys had to ride into the floating mass of cattle and try to get them moving to the bank. Some only survived after falling in the water, by holding on to a longhorn's or a horse's tail and being dragged ashore.

Questions

1. What qualities were needed to be a successful cowboy?
2. Look at the cowboy's working clothes shown above. It is said that everything he wore or carried was necessary and a good many things served more than one purpose. Taking this into consideration answer the following:
   (a) Suggest all the reasons a cowboy would have for wearing a wide-brimmed hat.
   (b) Suggest three different uses for the bandana.
   (c) Why would cowboys wear chaps?
   (d) Why did cowboys wear boots that had pointed toes and high heels? (You can find a clue to this answer by remembering that a cowboy spent most of his life on horseback.)

The trail crew

A modern historian has described the trail crew as follows:

After breakfast the trail boss rode off to look for water holes on either side of the trail, and to select the next camp site... Once the trail boss had decided on the next evening's camp site, the cook and his chuckwagon followed.

... Each trail rider had his position on the column – and he kept to it like a soldier going into battle. At either side of the head of the column were two point or lead riders... They scouted, tested fords, and directed the cattle...

Behind the point riders came the swing men, who took the place of a point rider if he rode ahead. The flank riders were next. These men rode close to the herd ... their job was to patrol the column constantly, drive stragglers back, and scare off foreign cattle.

At the rear were the drag or tail drivers ... they forced weak tail-enders to keep pace, and kept the column orderly ... Another of their jobs was to stop the cattle from bunching. Steers jammed together generated heat which lost them pounds in weight. (4)

Exercise
Draw a diagram to explain how the cowboys controlled the herd during the trail drive. Mark in the position of the trail boss, swing men, point riders, drag men, flank men and chuck wagon.

Nat Love, a negro cowboy. In a typical trail crew of eight cowboys at least two would be black

There were usually between 1 000 and 2 000 cattle in a herd with a trail crew of 6–12 riders, with a cook and a boy. The youngest boy was often the wrangler, that is, he was in charge of the horse herd. The cook was in charge of the mobile canteen, called the chuck wagon. The cook would prepare dishes like beans and salt pork, or pancakes and biscuits. Beans were served sometimes three times a day.

One real-life cowboy, Matt Hinkle, wrote:

As I muse over my past life it occurs to me that possibly more has been written about the American cowboy, more has been said, more moving-pictures made of and about him, than any other character in American history. I am proud to have been one of those early-day cowboys. He is the most romantic, most glamorised and most misunderstood figure ever to ride across the pages of our history. (5)

Questions
1 Why do you think that the life of the cowboy has been made to seem so glamorous by films and television?
2 If you were trying to give a true picture of cowboy life what facts would you mention which show that his life was far from glamorous?
3 Read again the section called 'Changes in the cowboy's life' which can be found in chapter 7. Use this and the present chapter to write or plan an interview with a cowboy explaining the changes he has seen taking place in cattle ranching between 1860 and 1890 and commenting on the good and bad effects of the changes on his way of life. You might like to make a tape of the interview.
4 We still use cowboy words today. Find out what each of the following means: lynch, posse and corral.

9 THE HOMESTEADERS

Thousands upon thousands of ... wagons had travelled through the great central prairies and plains before pioneers thought of actually settling there. And, indeed, the vast region abounded in reasons for pressing on. It was treeless ... very dry farther west, and everywhere possessed of a climate that ran to brutal extremes of hot and cold. But after the Civil War (1861–65), pioneers swarmed on to this desolate expanse – and stayed. In two decades more new US land was brought under cultivation than in the previous two and a half centuries. (1)

The white people on the Great Plains 1840–90

Date	Progress of settlement
1840s	Pioneers journeyed over the Great Plains in their covered wagons to California and Oregon.
1860–80	Cattle ranchers and cowboys moved from south and west on to the plains.
1854–65	First farmers settled on prairie grasslands on eastern edge of the Great Plains. They grew maize and vegetables because of the rich brown soil and fairly dependable rainfall.
1865–90	Settlers moved on to the drier lands of the central and western parts of the Great Plains.

See also the map on page 24

Why did so many people after 1865 move on to unsuitable farm land? One man wrote:

... the deciding motive ... was the lure of land that could be had practically without money... Land was a mighty motive to a man who had sons growing to manhood. He wanted them to have the opportunity of taking nearby lands and settling on farms around him. (2)

Many foreigners were persuaded to leave their country and settle in the USA. Promises of cheap and fertile land fell on ready ears of land-starved Germans and Scandinavians, and poor English farmers who were struggling to make ends meet. Exaggerated newspaper reports were used to attract people. The *Coolidge Border Ruffian* reported in July 1886:

Is it good country for corn, you ask? Stranger, you'll never know what a corn country is until you go to Kansas. When the husking is done in the Autumn the men go out with mallets and wedges and split up the corn-stalks for shipment to the East as telegraph poles. (3)

Railroad companies played a great part in luring settlers to the West. By selling land to settlers they could raise money to pay for the building of the railroad. Furthermore the greater the number of farms and towns set up the greater would be the business for the railroad.

Many settlers were attracted by the thought of free land after 1862. During that year the Homestead Act was passed. This allowed settlers to claim 65 hectares (160 acres) of free land if they lived and worked on it for five years.

Railway advertisement for prairie land

Questions

1. Explain why the homesteaders moved west.
2. Produce a poster or newspaper article designed to attract homesteaders to the Great Plains after 1860.
3. Look closely at the advertisement and extract 1. In what ways do they give a different impression of the region? Why do you think the poster makes the prairies sound so attractive?

The problems of the new settlers

After claiming their land the first job for the new homesteaders was to build a shelter. Those in the very dry central and western parts were forced to use the only building material available: sods of prairie grass. Some settlers made themselves dug-outs, but these had disadvantages:

The dugouts were made by digging into the hillsides or banks. They were reasonably dry and storm-proof and kept cool in summer and warm in winter. But dirt continuously fell from the roof. Animals, snakes and birds tunnelled into the walls and roof. Cattle sometimes unwittingly wandered on to the roof and crashed down into the house. (4)

So dugouts were unpleasant, and soon houses were being built from turf:

Sod houses were built from blocks of turf about 15–20 inches (38–51 cm) long, 12–15 inches (30–38 cm) wide and 2–4 inches (5–10 cm) thick... The roof was supported by timber which also composed the window frames and door... Sod houses were lighter and better ventilated than dugouts. Inside they were often plastered with a

Settlers outside their sod house

mixture of sand and clay. When dry it was whitewashed and the interior was more pleasant to live in. Nevertheless, dirt and dust filtered through and heavy rain storms could ruin walls and roof and cause their collapse. (5)

The climate was harsh:

Summer droughts, when the thermometer rose well above 100° (38°C) and hovered there for weeks on end, could char a pioneer's corn crop as effectively as a blowtorch. In winter, when temperatures sometimes plunged to 40° below zero (−40°C), horrendous snowstorms struck so suddenly that a man might lose his way between his house and barn and freeze to death. And there was the wind. It blew ceaselessly – winter and summer, night and day – a low moan that drove many pioneers to distractions. (6)

The ground was tough: 'An ordinary plough would often snag in the sod or skitter across its surface like a stick over ice.' Gathering in the harvest was long and back-breaking work since there were no casual labourers to help, and mechanical harvesters were too expensive. Cattle strayed on to the crops because of the lack of timber for fencing, and the low rainfall meant that the crop yield was not big enough. Most pioneers, in fact, only found water by digging – often to incredible depths:

One man who each day carted his water in casks from a neighbour's well, a fair distance away, was asked why he didn't dig a well of his own. He replied that he would as soon go a mile in one direction as another. His estimate of a mile was an exaggeration, but some settlers had to sink shafts of 280 feet (85 m) or more before reaching underground water. (7)

Life was tough enough in ordinary circumstances, but in the 1860s there came droughts, and in the 1870s plagues of grasshoppers which devoured everything in their path and shattered the dreams of many families.

The Homestead Act, which at first sight seemed so advantageous to the farmer, was in fact one of his chief causes of difficulty. It attracted large numbers of settlers, but much of the best land had already been given to the railroads or to the governments of the new territories to build and finance schools and other public buildings. Loop-holes in the act meant that much of the remaining land was dishonestly claimed by land grabbers. In the end many farmers had little choice but to buy land or settle on the remaining poor land. Furthermore 65 hectares (160 acres) was too small an area for farming in a dry climate. Therefore, from 1873 the government allowed farmers to claim a further 65 hectares (160 acres) of free land if they planted 0.2 hectare (one half acre) of trees.

Questions
1 The Indians objected to the large number of whites who began to settle and fence the plains in the late 1860s. However, as you have read, the Indians were just one of the many problems faced by the homesteaders.
   Either (a) draw a cartoon to show some of the problems,
   or   (b) produce extracts from the diary you might have kept during your first year out on the plains. Your extracts should concentrate on the difficulties and dangers of this first year.
2 The Indians were not the only group of people who objected to the homesteaders fencing off the plains. Who was the other group of people, and why did they dislike the homesteaders' actions? (Chapter 7 will help you.)

New methods of farming

New problems in farming needed new methods of solution and in the 1880s ways were found to overcome the problems of shortage of labour, lack of timber and lack of water. Cheap, new improved inventions, like the mechanical reapers and threshers, meant that extra men were not needed. Windpumps made use of the constant prairie breeze to raise a continuous supply of water. The railway transported these new inventions to the prairies:

Windmills sprouted across the grasslands, and a lace-work of irrigation ditches crisscrossed the dry plains of Colorado and

Wyoming. A new kind of wheat, introduced in 1874 by ... immigrants from Russia ... proved hardy enough to withstand severe extremes of climate... Giant new machines (steel ploughs), and reapers and combines pulled by lumbering steam tractors, allowed a sod-buster to cultivate in one afternoon the same amount of acreage that would have taken him weeks to work by hand. Barbed-wire fences enabled him to protect his holding against intrusion (e.g. animals straying on to the crops)... (8)

Questions
1. How important were: (a) the railways, (b) barbed wire, (c) the windpump, in the settlement of the Great Plains by homesteaders?
2. Write an interview with *either* a farmer who has succeeded in building a new way of life on the Great Plains *or* a farmer who has failed and been forced to return to the eastern states.
3. The life of a homesteader's teenage daughter or son would be different from your life in some ways and like it in others. Write about the differences or likenesses under each of the following headings; (a) work; (b) social life; (c) hopes or fears for the future.

Women out west

In western films women often appear as 'extras' to the plot, as the glamorous prize who is won by the handsome hero when the gunsmoke has cleared away. In true life, however, the western woman worked extremely hard. Those who went west with their families had not only to cook, clean and look after the children but also take part in the farm work. They faced difficulties in performing even simple tasks: on parts of the prairies the only fuel available for cooking was cowchips, that is dung! There were other difficulties too:

Sometimes the hazards of nature could make a sensitive person's life a misery. As soon as a house was built far out on an isolated plain, a cloud of flies enveloped it ... the flies swarmed freely over dining tables and awakened sleepers before daybreak. Even worse than the flies were biting gnats. (9)

Centipedes and scorpions were a terror to women in the south-west. It was unsafe to place a bed closer than two feet from a wall, or one might awaken amongst a company of those pests. (10)

Women were rare in the west and often had to be persuaded to leave the east to provide wives for lonely men. The advent of family life on

Cowchips for fuel. Kansas in the 1880s

the frontier certainly changed life in the rough west, as the following extract shows:

> *When neighbours who had two attractive young daughters moved near Granville Stuart's ranch on the Montana frontier, the mens' manners and dress improved overnight. 'Every man in camp has shaved and changed his shirt' wrote Stuart. 'We are trying to behave like civilized men!' When Mrs Lang arrived on her husband's ranch, swearing almost disappeared, grooming improved, Sundays were observed for the first time and the men's diet was rounded out with milk, butter and vegetables.* (11)

The women in the western towns organised campaigns against drunkenness and gambling. Their influence helped make the West a more civilised place in which to live.

Question
The western historian Dee Brown has called his book on women in the Old West *The Gentle Tamers*. Explain why he may have chosen this name.

10 BILLY THE KID

Most of the thousands of people who flocked to the West were ordinary and law-abiding but there were outlaws. One of the most famous was Billy the Kid, and in this chapter we will try to find out what he was really like. In many American films he is something of a hero, and is portrayed by handsome actors. To some historians, however, he was simply a cruel killer.

Questions
1. Look at the photograph of the real Billy. Is he as handsome as the film-makers would like us to think?
2. The photograph of Billy is usually printed the wrong way round. Paul Newman played Billy in a film called *The Left-handed Gun*. What was wrong with this title?

Billy as he really was – right-handed. Most photographs of him are printed the wrong way round

Over 500 books have been written about Billy, many of them based on a book titled *An Authentic Life of Billy the Kid* (1882), written by Sheriff Pat Garrett who shot and killed Billy.

This extract mentions some of the claims in Garrett's book:

> Billy, aged twelve, had (killed) 'a filthy loafer' who had made an insulting remark about his mother, using a pocket knife, 'its blade dripping with gore' after the deed . . . how Billy once routed a band of Indians, his pistol belching forth 'a stream of death laden fire' . . . (1)

Other books claim that Billy single-handed tracked down five men who were involved in the killing of his friend, John Tunstall. All in all Billy was supposed to have killed 21 men in his lifetime.

The modern story

Modern historians have carefully searched through old newspapers and documents and come up with a very different story, which is summarised below. We take up the story when Billy is fourteen and working. His employer described him as:

> the only kid who ever worked here who never stole anything. (2)

To his teacher he was:

The book cover of an early version of Billy's life story

chores: jobs

> no more of a problem than any other boy, always quite willing to help with chores around the schoolhouse. (3)

39

Billy's first clash with the law was minor:

An older man, playing a joke on a Chinese laundryman, stole a bundle of clothes and got the ever-obliging Billy to hide it. A Silver City peace officer clapped the boy in jail just to teach him a lesson. (4)

Billy expected awful consequences to follow, and so escaped via a chimney for Arizona, where he worked quietly as a ranch hand; there he was first called the Kid, or Kid Antrim. Then on 17 August 1877 he killed his first man. A fight developed between the Kid and a nasty bully, Frank Cahill:

Cahill jumped on him and threw him to the ground. Like everybody else who made a claim – no matter how slender – to manhood, the Kid wore a gun. He pulled it and fired. 'He had no choice; he had to use his gun,' a witness said. Cahill died the next day, and the Kid was locked in the Camp Grant guardhouse. A few nights later he broke out and got away. (5)

Billy became a cowboy, and in 1877 was working for an Englishman, John Tunstall, who was an important Lincoln County rancher. Events were soon to take a dramatic turn:

Tunstall had set up in business as a trader with a man called McSween, and they were business rivals of another trader, Murphy. Tunstall was determined to get half of every dollar made in Lincoln County and Murphy was determined to stop him. Tunstall was murdered by Murphy's men and the story goes that the Kid swore revenge on the murderers. (6)

Before long the Kid and the other Tunstall men caught up with a Murphy man, Sheriff Brady. Brady died with 16 bullets in him. After more fighting, a battle took place round McSween's store in Lincoln. McSween and several others were killed and the store was set on fire. Billy escaped and took to cattle-rustling and horse-thieving. He tried to set up a deal with the Governor by which he would give evidence against other men who had killed with him, in return for a free pardon. The deal fell through.

He was also prepared to rob his fellow outlaws:

One of his cattle-rustling operations brought him a wad of 800 dollars from a Colorado beef-buyer. When it came time to share out the take, Billy the Kid peeled off 30 dollars for one of his [gang] 'because he had a family', and staked the other rustler to a new pair of boots. He kept the rest of the money. (7)

By now Billy and his gang were becoming a menace. He was arrested by Pat Garrett, once his friend and now a sheriff, and sentenced to await hanging in Lincoln County Courthouse. What happened next was to make all America ring with his name:

Billy kills Deputy Olinger while escaping

manacled: chained

He was manacled hand and foot and watched continually by Deputies Olinger and Bell, but his friends managed to smuggle a pistol into the washroom. One night, Olinger went across the road to have his supper. At once Billy asked to visit the washroom and clanked his way there. A minute later he returned with the gun and ordered Bell into a side room. The deputy made a run for it and got a bullet in the back which sent him crashing down the stairs dead. Billy hobbled to the armoury, grabbed Olinger's loaded shotgun and went to a second-floor window to see the other deputy hurrying back from his meal, alerted by the shots. 'Hullo, Bob', called Billy and blasted Olinger full of buckshot. (8)

Billy escaped, only to be tracked down three months later by Pat Garrett (July 1881) who shot him dead in a dark room.

Questions

1. It was Garrett's book which claimed that Billy had killed at the age of 12 and had once routed a band of Indians. Can you think of any reasons why Garrett might claim such things?
2. Make two large posters about Billy the Kid.
   (a) a WANTED notice. This must be true and contain a life-like description. It should emphasise how evil Billy the Kid is, so that people will give information to the sheriff.
   (b) an advertisement. The aim is to give a romantic and dashing impression of Billy. The purpose of the poster is to get sightseers to visit the Lincoln County Courthouse where Billy made his dramatic escape. You can include some of Garretts' stories. Extracts 1 and 5 will help you.
3. Would a modern historian agree with the following statements?
   (a) Billy was bad from the start (extracts 2 and 3).
   (b) Billy on his own tracked down the killers of Tunstall.
   (c) Billy was mean (extract 7).
   (d) Billy shot men in the back (extract 8).

11 THE PLAINS WARS

At first the white people had been quite happy for the Indians to roam the prairies, as to them it was just a great desert. But in the 1850s settlers and miners began to cross Indian territory on their way to California and Oregon (chapters 5 and 6). The miners, in particular, hunted the buffalo on which the Indians depended for survival. Even more serious, settlers began to build farms on the prairies.

The railroad companies were ready to build a line across the prairies to link east and west coast. The Indians were ready to stop this. The Cheyenne chief, Roman Nose, warned:

We will not have the wagons which make a noise (steam engines) in the hunting grounds of the buffalo. If the palefaces come farther into our land, there will be scalps of your brethren in the wigwams of the Cheyennes. I have spoken. (1)

The Sand Creek Affair

With railway crews killing buffalo for meat, the Indians started attacking the white men. In 1864 Colonel John Chivington took full revenge for the years of Cheyenne and Arapaho raids on mining

Clearing the track of buffalo. William Cody was employed by the Kansas Pacific Railway Company to supply meat to the building crews. He killed 4 280 animals in seventeen months and earned the nickname 'Buffalo Bill'

camps, mail coaches and settlers. At Sand Creek two peaceful Cheyenne tribes, led by Chiefs Black Kettle and White Antelope, had set up their winter camp. Chivington planned to attack them:

Damn any man who sympathises with Indians. I have come to kill Indians and believe it is right and honourable to use any means under God's heaven to kill Indians. (2)

When some of his men protested that the Indian camp was mainly full of women and children, Chivington replied:

Kill and scalp all, big and small; nits make lice. (3)

Of the 133 Indians killed, 105 were women and children. A major in the US Army later reported:

Colonel J. M. Chivington, with the third regiment of Colorado cavalry attacked the camp of friendly Indians, the major portion of which were composed of women and children. Every one whom I have spoken to agrees that the most fearful atrocities were committed; women and children were killed and scalped; children shot at their mothers' breast, and all the bodies (cut) in the most horrible manner. Knowing that these Indians had been promised protection by myself and Major S. J. Anthony, he kept his command in ignorance of this. Colonel Chivington reports that between 500 and 600 Indians were left dead on the field. I have been informed by Captain Booth that he visited the field and counted 69 bodies...' (4)

The verdict of the *Denver News* on the Sand Creek Massacre was:

All acquitted themselves well. Colorado soldiers have again covered themselves with glory. (5)

Questions
1 What words in extract 4 suggest that Black Kettle was (a) peaceful and (b) not likely to have expected an attack.
2 Why might Colonel Chivington claim a far higher number of dead Indians than was true?
3 From what you know about Chivington do you think he would have encouraged a massacre?
4 What is your opinion of the verdict of the *Denver News*?

Red Cloud's war

The most dramatic of the many wars that followed soon after Sand Creek was Red Cloud's war, which the Indians won. We shall follow

The Bozeman Trial

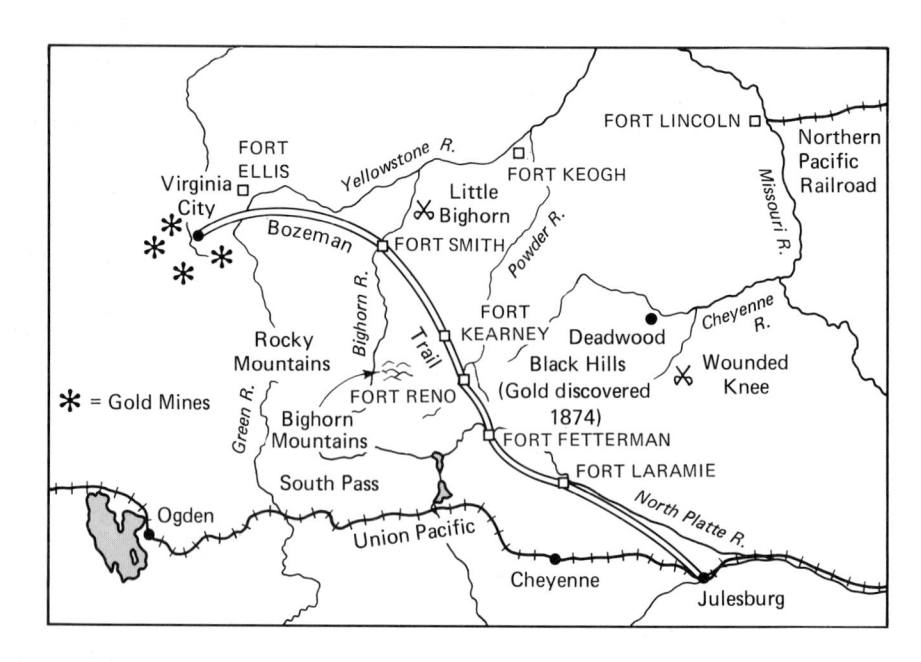

the fortunes of the Sioux in this and later chapters. The war was triggered off by the Bozeman Trail which ran from Julesburg to the goldfields of Montana. To the miners it was a vital route for their supplies, but Black Elk, Holy Man of the Oglala Sioux, had a different point of view:

> *The Wasichus (whitemen) had found much of the yellow metal that they worship and that makes them crazy and they wanted to have a road up through our country to the place where the yellow metal was. But my people did not want the road: it would scare the bison (buffalo) and make them go away and also it would let the other Wasichus come in like a river. And so, when the soldiers came and built themselves a town of logs (Fort Reno), my people knew that they meant to have their road and take our country and maybe kill us all when they were strong enough. Crazy Horse was only 19 then and Red Cloud was still our Greatest Chief.* (6)

The Sioux under Red Cloud went on the warpath. The army tried to build a series of forts along the road to protect travellers against Indian raids. However, under constant attack, they managed to build only two. In December 1866, Crazy Horse and his warriors wiped out 81 soldiers under the command of Captain W. Fetterman. The government knew it could not defeat the Indians without spending much more money and using many more men. The Indians were skilled horsemen, brave, and by now using guns. Red Cloud would only make peace if the whites closed down the Bozeman Trail and its forts. So successful had been Red Cloud's campaigns that the government agreed. Under the Treaty of Fort Laramie, November 1868, the Sioux were allowed to keep all their hunting grounds, including the Black Hills:

Red Cloud

The United States hereby agrees ... that the country north of the North Platte River and east of the summits of the Bighorn Mountains shall be Indian Territory, and also ... agrees that no white persons shall be permitted to settle upon or occupy any portion of (it); and it is further agreed by the United States, that within ninety days after the conclusion of peace with the Sioux Nation, the military posts now established in this territory shall be abandoned, and that the road leading to them and by them to the settlements in the Territory of Montana shall be closed. (7)

It was a great victory for the Indians, but within a few years Red Cloud was persuaded to agree to live on a reservation. The reservation was to be land set aside for the Indians, and supposedly free from white people. On the reservation the United States government would provide food, clothing and housing. The Indians would be taught to farm and in exchange would agree to remain on the reservation, leaving it only for buffalo hunting. Red Cloud visited the President of the United States in Washington for negotiations. While there he saw the huge guns in the US Arsenal and Navy Yard, and he could not have failed to realise how much stronger the whites were in both armaments and population. Red Cloud realised that, given the strength of the whites, they were unlikely to keep to the treaty. Many Indians also saw that their numbers were too small and their hunting grounds too big to defend themselves against a flood of white settlers with their railways and guns. Many more, however, did not wish to live on reservations. Food was short on the reservation and farming was regarded as women's work.

Then in 1874 George Armstrong Custer, 'Long Hair' as the Indians called him, led an expedition to the Black Hills. Black Elk described its results:

fall: autumn
rubbed out: killed

He had no right to go there because all that country was ours. Also the Wasichus had made a treaty with Red Cloud (1868) that said it would be ours as long as grass should grow and water flow. Later I learned too that Long Hair had found there much ... yellow metal ... In the fall we heard that some Wasichus had come from the Black Hills for the yellow metal because Long Hair had told them about it with a voice that went everywhere. Later he got rubbed out for doing that. (8)

Questions
1 What was the yellow metal referred to in extract 8?
2 Did the Treaty of Fort Laramie (extract 7) permit the white settlers to go and dig in the Black Hills for metal? (The map on page 44 will help you to find the places described.)

Within a year miners were rushing to the area. More and more Sioux refused to follow Red Cloud to the reservation (remember that chiefs could only advise and not order their warriors) and joined Crazy Horse, Sitting Bull and the other chiefs who would not accept any treaty with the whites.

The army decided the only way to safeguard the miners would be to confine and limit all the Indians to the reservation. In December 1875 an order was issued which said that all Indians who were not on the reservation by 31 January would be considered hostile. Some did as they were told, some never heard the order. Others like Crazy Horse and Sitting Bull prepared for war. They were joined by the Cheyenne. The stage was set for the most famous Indian battle of them all.

Questions
1 Imagine you are Crazy Horse. Make up a speech to deliver to your tribe giving the reasons why you intend to fight the white settlers and drive them out of your homeland.
2 Imagine you are Red Cloud. Give your reasons for agreeing to go on to the reservation.

12 BATTLE OF THE LITTLE BIGHORN

With many Indians refusing to go back to the reservation there was no alternative but to call in the army. Army scouts reported that the Indians were in the wild and rugged Bighorn Mountains. On 21 June 1876 two army columns, one led by Colonel Gibbon, the other by General Terry, met up at a planned point on the Yellowstone River. As part of his force General Terry had brought the fast-moving 7th Cavalry, led by George Armstrong Custer. General Terry was certain that the Sioux were camped in the valley of the stream known as the Little Bighorn. What General Terry did not know was that Crazy Horse and Sitting Bull had joined forces and been further strengthened by young warriors from Red Cloud's reservation as well as groups of Cheyenne and Arapaho: a total force of some 12 000.

General Terry's plan was that Colonel Gibbon and his troops would march south following the Bighorn river, while the 7th Cavalry would go around the southern end of the Wolf Mountains and then march north down the Little Bighorn river. The idea was that both Gibbon and Custer would attack the Indian camp at the same time from different directions. According to General Terry, Custer knew that Gibbon would not reach the Indian camp until the 26th. Gibbon's last words to Custer were 'Now, Custer, don't be greedy, wait for us'.

However, things do not go to plan. Without waiting for Colonel Gibbon, Custer attacked the Sioux on the 25th. According to one writer:

Custer was in desperate need of success. He was in trouble with the army authorities for disobedience and he thought that if he were a national hero, he might gain the office of President of the USA. Once near the Sioux, he refused to believe that he could not defeat any number of Indians. He divided his forces so that no Indians would escape him and with 215 men he rode at the enemy.

For once the Indians stood and fought. They attacked persistently. Custer fought a good defensive action... Custer was never a coward... He went down outnumbered something like six to one. Captain Benteen in charge of the bigger of the other sections of the 7th, refused to ride to the rescue, realising it was too late and that he had no chance against such odds... (1)

No white soldier survived the Little Bighorn so we do not know exactly what happened. Ever since 1876 people have argued about it. Some say Custer was a hero who fought bravely against overwhelming numbers. Some believe he was unlucky. Others say he disobeyed General Terry's orders, acted foolishly and was only out to win glory

General Custer. Born in 1839, Custer made his name as a dashing and ambitious officer during the Civil War. In 1866 he became commander of the 7th Cavalry. He was already well known to the Indians as the leader of the Black Hills expedition (chapter 11) and as the man who led the attack on Black Kettle's winter camp. In this attack Custer had successfully divided his command into three. Generally regarded as ambitious and somewhat reckless, he knew that a dashing victory over the Indians would help his political career. When he attacked at the Little Bighorn he either did not know he was facing the greatest number of Indians ever assembled in one place, or he felt he could defeat them as he had done time after time in the past

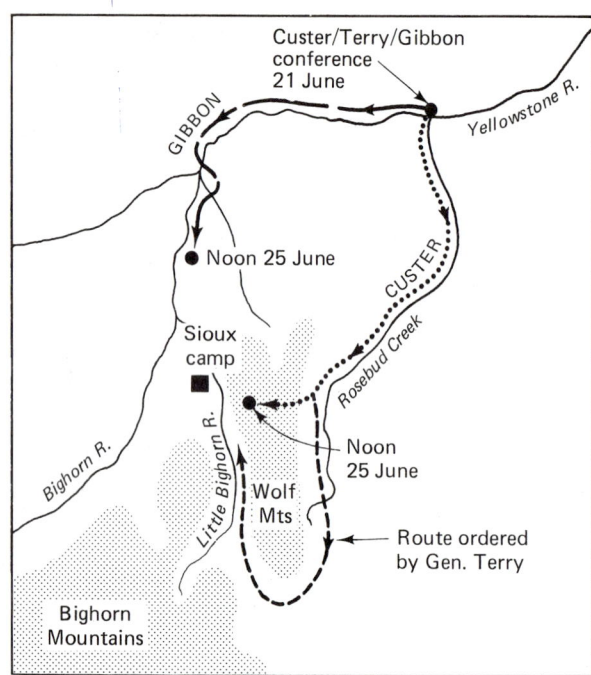

The movements of Custer and Gibbon from 21 June to noon 25 June. Note how Custer did not follow General Terry's orders

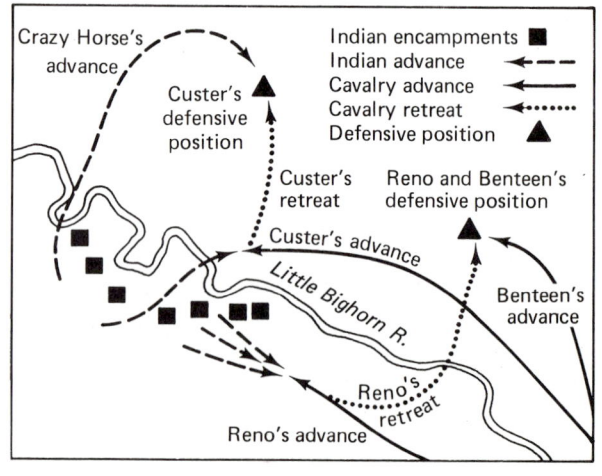

The battleground. Custer had split his men into three groups. The first group, under Benteen, was sent to scout the ridges; the second, under Reno, was to move directly forward. Custer led the third group. Reno met fierce resistance, retreated and was pinned down for a day or so. Benteen joined him later. Meanwhile Custer attacked, was pushed back, and found that another force, under Crazy Horse, had cut off his rear

Custer's Last Stand by Edgar Paxson, painted in 1899 after much research. Note that Custer's hair was not long, but regulation army length. Nobody knows at what stage of the battle Custer was killed, or who killed him. It may be that he killed himself since his blond hair remained intact and it is known that Indians did not scalp or interfere with the body of a suicide. Saving the last shot for yourself was not an uncommon practice when overwhelmed by Indians

for himself. Before you make a decision look very carefully at the illustrations and read the following extracts which try to explain why Custer attacked the village on his own without waiting for help:

Seeing the women and children fleeing from the village away from the approach of Major Reno, Custer thought the village had been caught unguarded, and that the victory would be an easy one. (2)

He thought, I am confident, that the Indians were running. For fear that they might get away he attacked without getting all his men... (General Terry's report to General Sheridan) (3)

It was common belief that the Sioux would, upon the appearance of the troops, hasten to strike their camp and escape. Nobody entertained the thought that they would stand and fight a pitched battle. That was not the Indian way. (4)

Questions

1. What motive is suggested by extract 1 for Custer's attack?
2. Is there anything in the extracts that might make us think that Custer simply made a mistake? Explain your answer.
3. Why might Custer have thought that the Indians would panic and flee, rather than fight, at the sight of his troops?
4. Is there any evidence to suggest that Custer may have been over-confident?
5. Why do you think the Indians won the Battle of Little Bighorn? Try looking in other books for more information.

When the news reached the eastern states the public demanded revenge, and plans were made to crush the Sioux once and for all. Sitting Bull fled to Canada with many of his followers, but they returned and surrendered in 1881 because of a shortage of food caused by the scarcity of buffalo. By then Crazy Horse had been murdered and Red Cloud forced to sell the Black Hills to the whites. Most Indians were now on the reservation. Why was there so little resistance left in the Sioux? One historian has written:

(In) 1876 the US Army underestimated the strength of the Sioux peoples ... (but after) the Little Bighorn (the army) threw everything into the war... The Sioux chiefs could obtain no guns and no fresh supplies of ammunition... They were given little peace to hunt and were forced to keep on the run as more and more soldiers swarmed into the land... (5)

The most important single cause, however, was the destruction of the buffalo herds by white hunters. Without a food supply the Indians could not go on fighting and had to move on to a reservation to be fed by the white authorities. Teddy 'Blue' Abbot, a cowboy, wrote in the 1880s:

That buffalo slaughter was a dirty business ... the hunters would round up a bunch of buffalo and shoot all down they could. The skinners would follow after in a wagon and take the hides. But when it got dark they would quit, leaving maybe ten or twenty carcasses ... they would just lie there on the prairie and rot, hides and all. It was all waste. All this slaughter was a put-up job on the part of the government to control Indians by getting rid of their food supply. But just the same it was a low-down dirty business. (6)

Sitting Bull

Questions
1. What reasons does the writer of extract 6 put forward for the slaughter of the buffalo? Does the writer agree or disagree with the slaughter? Give reasons.
2. Why was the slaughter of the buffalo so important in the final defeat of the Plains Indians?
3. What other reasons are suggested by extract 5 for the defeat of the Plains Indians?
4. Why can it be argued that the Battle of the Little Bighorn turned out badly for the Indians?

13 THE GHOST DANCE AND WOUNDED KNEE

Life on the reservation

Life on the reservation was hard for the Indians to accept:

> *If some evil genie would take us by the scruff of the neck, and take us into some strange world which we could neither understand nor leave, where we had to lead a life for which we were utterly unprepared, and where everything we had been taught was useless, we would find ourselves in the same situation that faced the Indians on the reservations.* (1)

Some white people thought that all the problems could be solved by giving the Indians a plot of land, some corn and some farm tools. However, they were wrong:

> *These good people forgot that the land set aside for the Indians was in most cases unsuitable for raising crops. They also ignored the fact that the Indians were brought up to look upon farming as women's work, shameful for a man to do even in some tribes that had at one time practised agriculture.* (2)

The Ghost Dance

In 1889 things started to go badly wrong. The Indian crops failed as a result of dry winds, a measles epidemic wiped out hundreds of their children, and their monthly beef rations were cut by half leading to starvation. In very low spirits, without hope and purpose, they were only too willing to believe the rumour of an Indian called Wovoka who preached that the Indians' own way of life would return:

> *A great flood would come, and the earth would roll itself up like a giant carpet. Rolled up would be the 'iron snake' and the 'whispering wire', the ugly smelters and mine dumps, the fences and the stinking new animals (pigs and sheep), the filthy towns with their saloons and gambling houses. Underneath would appear the new, happy world that the Great Spirit intended for his children, forever green and unspoiled.*
>
> *To these new plains would return the departed ones, the dead ancestors, the parents and children killed by war and famine. The tribes would live in peace and make war no more. The white man would disappear, go back to faraway lands across the Big Water.* (3)

On the reservation the Indians had to depend on the white man's government for food. These Indians are drawing rations from government agents

A Ghost shirt. The Indians believed it would turn away the white soldier's bullets

Questions
1 What do you think the 'iron snake' and the 'whispering wire' were (extract 3)?
2 Is Wovoka encouraging the Indians to go back on the warpath?

Convinced by Wovoka, the Indians believed that all they had to do for their dreams to come true was dance the Ghost Dance. The dancers wore shirts painted with special religious markings. Some tribes believed these would protect them from bullets.

Wounded Knee

The ranchers and homesteaders living near the reservation were worried. They thought the Indians were going to go on the warpath again. In fact, Wovoka's message was peaceful, but on 15 December

1890 Sitting Bull, the Sioux leader, was shot dead by two Indian police who had been ordered to place him under arrest. He was wrongly seen as one of the leading figures in the Ghost Dance affair. The Sioux were now angry and frightened and many scattered. One group, led by Big Foot, was caught by the soldiers and escorted to a small settlement called Wounded Knee. The soldiers said the Indians must give up their weapons:

> *The search produced only two old guns. The officer knew there were more and sent scouts and soldiers to search. One of the medicine men tried to stir up the men against the soldiers. Some of the young men took guns from under their blankets and fired at the soldiers who fired back.* (4)

The soldiers had previously placed four machine guns on a rise overlooking the tepees. These now opened fire. Louise Weasel Bear remembered:

> *We tried to run but they shot us like we were buffalo. I know there are some good white people, but the soldiers must be mean to shoot children and women. Indian soldiers would not do that to white children.* (5)

Hand-to-hand fighting then developed. The bodies of the dead and dying were found scattered over the snow for a distance of three miles. 84 warriors, including Big Foot, 44 women and 18 children died at once. At least 33 more were wounded, some of whom died later:

Indians heaped into mass graves after Wounded Knee

> *On New Year's Day 1891, three days after the killings, the dead Indians were buried naked in a long pit. Their Ghost shirts were*

ripped off them by souvenir hunters. The Sioux no longer believed in Wovoka and the coming of the new world. At Wounded Knee lay buried not only many Indians but the hopes and dreams of the whole Sioux nation. (6)

The remaining Sioux finally surrendered to the army in 1891. Other tribes suffered similar fates and eventually all the Indians were confined to reservations.

For class discussion
Chief Red Cloud said: 'The white man made us many promises, more than I can remember, but they never kept but one; they promised to take our land, and they took it.'
Do you think you would have felt the same way if you had been an Indian at this time? (You may need to refresh your memory by looking at chapters 11 and 12).

Further research
Many Indian tribes suffered a similar fate to the Sioux. Use reference books to find out all you can about how the following tribes and their leaders stood up against the white intruders. In each case try to work out why they were eventually defeated:
(a)   The Apaches, led by Cochise and Geronimo.
(b)   The Nez Percés, led by Chief Joseph.

intruders: people who push in where they are not wanted

The end of the West

By 1900 the West was no longer the centre of attraction. There were few areas of land still to settle, and farming was no longer the main activity of America. Large industries and cities were rising in the East. The days of the settler, the cowboy, the Indian, and the outlaw were over. Taking their place were inventors, scientists, bankers, industrialists and factory workers.

Today, many Americans yearn for the freedom and adventure of the Old West. None more so than the modern Indians who are still on their reservations:

Probably for most of the Plains Indians today, the real dream is to be back on the prairie. They may drive a car but they wish it were a horse. They may live in a house but they wish it were a tepee. They may dance to a jukebox but they wish it were a drum – beating slowly, pounding out the Sun Dance, willing the buffalo to return. (7)

INDEX

Numerals in **bold** denote illustrations

Arapaho, 7, 12, 42, 47

barbed wire, 28, **28**, 37
Big Foot, 5, **5**, 53
Bighorn Mountains, 45, 47, **48**
Billy the Kid, 39–41, **39**, **41**
Black Hills, 23, 44, 46, 50
Bozeman Trail, 44, **44**
buffalo, 8–9, **9**, 12, 15, 24, 42, **42**, 45, 50, 54
'Buffalo Bill', 42

California trail, 17, **18**, 20, 33
cattlemen, 23, 24–8, **28**, 33
cattle trails, 25, 26, **26**
Cheyenne, 7, 12, 15, 42, 43, 46, 47
Chivington, Colonel John, 42–3
Comanche, 7, 12, 13
cowboys, 24, 25, 26, 27, 28–32, **28**, **29**, **30**, **31**, **32**, 33, 40, 50
Crazy Horse, 44, 46, 47, **48**, 50
Custer, George Armstrong, 46, 47–9, **48**, **49**

'dog soldiers', 15

Fetterman massacre, 44
Fort Laramie, Treaty of, 44–5

Garrett, Pat, 39, 40, 41
Ghost Dance, 51–2, **52**, 53
Gibbon, Colonel, 47, **48**
Gold Rush, California, 20–3
    effect of, 23
    miner's life, 21–2, **22**
    routes, 19–20, **20**
Great Plains, 10, 12, 24, **24**, 27, 33

Homesteaders, 33–8
    conflict with cattlemen, 28
    Homestead Act, 34, 36
    problems of, 34–7, **35**, **38**
horses, 12, 13, 14, 15, **16**, 29, **29**, 31, 32, 40, 54

Indians, 7–16
    arrival of, 7
    beliefs of, 10–11
    bravery, 12–13, 14, 15
    sign language, 10, **10**
Iroquois, 8

Lewis and Clark, **6**
Little Big Horn, Battle of, 47–50, **48**, **49**
Longhorn cattle, 24–5, **24**, 31
Louisiana Purchase, **6**

Medicine Men, 4, 14, 53
Mexico, 17, 19, 24
Mormons, 17

Nez Percé, **7**, 11, 12

open range, 27–8, 29
Oregon trail, 17, **18**, 33

Plains Indians, 12–16
    childhood, 14
    elderly, 14–15
    government, 15
    methods of warfare, 13
    pastimes, **16**
    religion, 14
    struggle with whiteman, 42–54
prairies, 8, 9, 11, 12, 23, 26, 27, 33, **34**, 36, 37, 42, 50, 54

railroad, 23, 25, 26, 34, **34**, 36, 42
Red Cloud, 43–6, **45**, **47**, 50
reservations, 5, **5**, 45, 46, 50, 51, **51**, 52

Sand Creek Affair, 42–3
scalping, 13
Sioux, 8, 9, 10, 12, **13**, 15, **16**, 44, 45, 46, 49, 50, 53, 54
Sitting Bull, 46, 47, 50, **50**, 53
sod houses, 34–5, **35**
stampede, 30–1, **30**
Sun Dance, 14, **14**, 54

tepee, 9, **9**, 10, **10**, 14, 54
Terry, General, 47, 49
Texas, **6**, 24–5, **24**, 28, 29
trail crews, 31–2

wagon trains, 17–18, **19**
windmills and windpumps, 28, **28**, 36, **36**
women, 37–8, **38**
Wounded Knee, 5, 5, 6, 52–4, **53**

55

Sources

2 The first Americans
1 B W Beacroft and M A Smale, *The Making of America* (Longman 1972)
2 C Davis, *A Closer Look at the Plains Indians* (Archon Press 1977)
3 Chief Luther Standing Bear, *Land of the Spotted Eagle* (Houghton and Mifflin, 1933)
4 D McLoughlin, *The Encyclopedia of the Old West* (Routledge and Kegan Paul, 1977)
5 and 6 B Capps, *The Indians* (Time-Life, 1973)
7 D Brown, *Bury my Heart at Wounded Knee* (Holt, Reinhart and Winston, New York 1970)
8 H A Howard, *War Chief Joseph* (Caxton, 1941)
9 H Greeley, *An Overland Journey from New York to San Francisco in the Summer of 1859* (Knopf, 1964)

3 Plains Indians – warfare
1 K Ulyatt, *The Time of the Indians* (Penguin, 1975)
2 V Luting, *Indians of the North American Plains* (Macdonald Educational, 1978)
3 G Mogridge, *The Indians of North America* (Religious Society Tract, 1853)
4 Jon Manchip White, *Everyday Life of the North American Indian* (Batsford, 1979)

4 Plains Indians – home life
1 and 2 Chief Luther Standing Bear, *Land of the Spotted Eagle* (Houghton Mifflin, 1933)
3 John G Neihardt (ed.), *Black Elk Speaks* (Abacus/Sphere, 1974)
4 R I Dodge, *The Hunting Grounds of the Great West* (Chatto and Windus, 1877)

5 The white settlers move west
1 Huston Horn, *The Pioneers* (Time-Life, 1974)
2 John A Hawgood, *The American West* (Eyre and Spottiswoode, 1967)
3 Alistair Cooke, *America* (BBC Publications, 1973)
4 George R Stewart, *The California Trail* (Eyre and Spottiswoode, 1962)

6 The California Gold Rush
1 Joan Chandler, *The Settlement of the American West* (OUP)
2 D Lavender, *The Penguin Book of the American West* (Penguin, 1969)
3 R A Billington, *The Far Western Frontier 1830–60* (Harper and Row, 1965)
4 Schools Council, *The American West 1840–95* (Holmes McDougall, 1977)

7 The cattlemen
1 and 4 K Ulyatt, *The Day of the Cowboy* (Puffin, 1973)
2 J McCoy, *Historic Sketches of the Cattle Trade of the West and South West* (Ralph P. Bieber ed.; Southwest Historical series no. 5; 1940)
3 B W Beacroft and M A Smale, *The Making of America* (Longman, 1972)
5 Granville Stuart, *Forty Years on the Frontier*

8 The life of a cowboy
1 Ramon Adams, *The Old Time Cowhand* (Macmillan, New York, 1961)
2 and 3 Robin May and Joseph G Rosa, *Cowboy – The Man and the Myth* (NEL, 1980)
4 and 11 Marlboro, *The Real Cowboy* (Barrie and Jenkins, 1975)
5 *True West Magazine* (Western Publications Inc, 1961)

9 The homesteaders
1, 6, 7 and 8 Huston Horn, *Pioneers in the American West* (Time-Life, 1974)
2 *Narratives of Noah Harris Letts and Thomas Allen Banning 1823–1863* (Lakeside Press, 1972)
3 R W Richmond and R W Mardock, *A Nation Moving West* (University of Nebraska, 1966)
4 and 5 B W Beacroft and M A Smale, *The Making of America* (Longman, 1972)
9 and 10 Dee Brown, *The Gentle Tamers* (Barrie and Jenkins, 1973)

10 Billy the Kid
1 Joseph Rosa and Robin May, *Gunsmoke: A Study of Violence in the Wild West* (NEL, 1977)
2, 3, 4 and 5 Paul Trachtman, Quoted in *The Gunfighters* (Time-Life, 1974)
6 Barbara Currie, *Railroads and Cowboys in the American West* (Longman, 1974)
7 Quoted in *Daily Telegraph Colour Supplement* November 21, 1975
8 Robin May, *The Wild West* (Independent Television Books, 1975)

11 The Plains Wars
1 Charles H L Johnson, *Famous Indian Chiefs* (L C Page, 1909)
2 and 3 Michael Gibson, Quoted in *The American Indian* (Wayland, 1974)
4 and 5 R W Richmond and R W Mardock, Quoted in *A Nation Moving West* (University of Nebraska Press, 1966)
6 and 8 John G Neihardt (ed.), *Black Elk Speaks* (Abacus/Sphere, 1974)
7 C J Kappler, *Indian Treaties 1778–1883* (Interland Publishing Inc., 1972)

12 Battle of the Little Bighorn
1 Matt Chisholm, Quoted in *The True Book of the Wild West* (Hampton House Productions, 1978)
2 and 5 Stephen White, Quoted in *All About Plains Indians* (W H Allen, 1975)
3 W A Graham, *The Story of the Little Bighorn: Custer's Last Fight* (Stackpole Company, 1926)
4 C Neider, Quoted in *The Great West* (Bonanza Books, 1958)
6 E C Abbott and H H Smith, *We Pointed Them North* (University of Oklahoma Press, 1966)

13 The Ghost Dance and Wounded Knee
1, 2 and 3 Richard Erdoes, *The Sun Dance People* (Ronald Stacy, 1973)
4 Barbara Currie, *Railroads and Cowboys in the American West* (Longman, 1974)
5 J H McGregor, *The Wounded Knee Massacre from the Viewpoint of the Survivors* (Wirth Brothers, 1940)
6 B W Beacroft, *The Last Fighting Indians of the American West* (Longman, 1976)
7 Christopher Davis, *A Closer Look at the Plains Indians* (Archon Press, 1977)